Dear Mary

I hope you enjoy
the book. It's been
a great experience!
Here's hoping you
find "truth" in
all you do!

love
Isabelle

P.S. Sorry it took so
long to get to you!

The 4Cs

of Truth in Communications

MARKETING BOOKS FROM PMP

MARKET RESEARCH

Consumer Insights 2.0: *How Smart Companies Apply Customer Knowledge to the Bottom Line*

Dominators, Cynics, and Wallflowers: *Practical Strategies for Moderating Meaningful Focus Groups*

Moderating to the Max! *A Full-Tilt Guide to Creative, Insightful Focus Groups and Depth Interviews*

The Mirrored Window: *Focus Groups from a Moderator's Point of View*

Religion in a Free Market: *Religious and Non-Religious Americans—Who, What, Why, Where*

Why People Buy Things They Don't Need

MATURE MARKET/ BABY BOOMERS

After Fifty: *How the Baby Boom Will Redefine the Mature Market*

After Sixty: *Marketing to Baby Boomers Reaching Their Big Transition Years*

Advertising to Baby Boomers

Marketing to Leading-Edge Baby Boomers

The Boomer Heartbeat: *Capturing the Heartbeat of the Baby Boomers Now and in the Future*

MULTICULTURAL

Beyond Bodegas: *Developing a Retail Relationship with Hispanic Customers*

Hispanic Marketing Grows Up: *Exploring Perceptions and Facing Realities*

Marketing to American Latinos: *A Guide to the In-Culture Approach, Part I*

Marketing to American Latinos: *A Guide to the In-Culture Approach, Part II*

The Whole Enchilada: *Hispanic Marketing 101*

What's Black About It? *Insights to Increase Your Share of a Changing African-American Market*

YOUTH MARKETS

The Kids Market: *Myths & Realities*

Marketing to the New Super Consumer: Mom & Kid

The Great Tween Buying Machine: *Marketing to Today's Tweens*

MARKETING MANAGEMENT

A Clear Eye for Branding: *Straight Talk on Today's Most Powerful Business Concept*

A Knight's Code of Business: *How to Achieve Character and Competence in the Corporate World*

Beyond the Mission Statement: *Why Cause-Based Communications Lead to True Success*

India Business: *Finding Opportunities in this Big Emerging Market*

Marketing Insights to Help Your Business Grow

The 4Cs

of Truth in Communications

How to Identify, Discuss, Evaluate
and Present Stand-out,
Effective Communication

Isabelle Albanese

PARAMOUNT MARKET PUBLISHING, INC.

Paramount Market Publishing, Inc.
950 Danby Road, Suite 136
Ithaca, NY 14850
www.paramountbooks.com
Telephone: 607-275-8100; 888-787-8100   Facsimile: 607-275-8101

Publisher: James Madden
Editorial Director: Doris Walsh

Cataloging in Publication Data available
ISBN-13: 978-0-9786602-2-2

Contents

Foreword

The core theories of marketing are not particularly complicated. Marketers need to clearly identify a target customer, differentiate their product and set pricing relative to the benefits provided. Few people are confused by the segment-targeting-positioning framework. The 4Ps are easy to remember: price, product, promotion, and place.

Nonetheless, many people and organizations struggle terribly with marketing, creating advertising and promotion campaigns that make surprisingly little sense and do almost nothing to drive sales and build the brand.

This is the great paradox of marketing. If it all is so simple, why is it so hard?

One reason why marketing is harder than it seems is that great marketing requires both strategy and creativity. It isn't enough to figure out the perfect strategy. For a marketing campaign to work, the strategy has to be turned into a marketing program, the tangible manifestations of the strategy. In many cases this is a piece of communication, such as advertising or promotions.

Many marketers are far more comfortable with strategy than creativity. I have taught marketing at Northwestern

University's Kellogg School of Management for almost a decade. During that time I have noticed that most marketing students are very comfortable dealing with strategic issues and financial analyses; there are numbers to work with and formulas to apply. Students are often uncomfortable, however, with softer issues such as creativity and communication; the topics are gray and subjective and ultimately intangible. For many marketers, it is easier to figure out what needs to be said, than to actually sort out how to say it.

That is why *The 4Cs of Truth in Communication* is such a valuable book; it provides a simple, clear, and easy to use framework for creating powerful creative. It can help a marketer bridge the often imposing gap between strategy and creative.

The 4Cs framework is startling in its simplicity. That, of course, is the power; it is easy to remember and easy to use. The 4Cs framework can lead to better creative executions, and better creative executions will lead to stronger business results.

Before joining the Kellogg School of Management faculty, I spent eleven years as a marketing executive at Kraft Foods, managing a variety of different brands. During that time I had the opportunity to work with Isabelle Albanese. Together we created a series of advertising campaigns that resonated with consumers and ultimately built the brand and the business. Isabelle played a critical role in the process; she was able to listen to the consumer and identify the insights that directly led to the advertising. She has an uncanny knack for listening to consumers and figuring out what is important. In this book she shares her approach in a practical, witty, direct style.

Ultimately, marketing is about communication. To build a brand and build a business, a marketer has to be able to create powerful communication pieces. This book is an invaluable tool for doing just that.

TIM CALKINS
Clinical Professor of Marketing
Kellogg School of Management
Northwestern University

Acknowledgements

I am truly thankful for the opportunity to have written this book, which has been a wonderfully exciting and fulfilling experience, and which would not have been possible without:

God, from whom I have derived my strength, stamina and enlightenment, and all inspiration that is good and truthful

My husband and business partner, Ken Quaas, from whom comes an amazing amount of love, support, patience and encouragement. He is my life partner in every way.

My children—Julianne, Matthew, and John—from whom comes and to whom flows the greatest love and the greatest truths! They can always be counted on to help me keep it all in perspective.

My mother, who keeps me grounded and has always dreamt big for me

My friend and writing partner, Mark Silveira, who has sweated this book out with me from day one

My good friend and project manager, Valerie Mandarino, who kept me clear-headed throughout the year of writing

Dawn Dingman—who, upon first seeing my presentation of The 4Cs said, "That's pretty cool. You should write a book on that!"

The coaches and staff at The Strategic Coach®—especially Theresa Easler—who gave me the "push" to get on with it and the confidence to know I could.

And last but definitely NOT least, my clients—many of whom I consider my dear friends—and all of whom I value, respect, and "C" truth in every day. Thanks especially to Regina Lewis, Kelly Gronlund, Lisa McLean, and Pamela Narins, each of whom I am proud to say has been a great partner in every way, and have been incredibly supportive for many years.

I am truly blessed and incredibly thankful to have all of you in my life.

Preface

Men occasionally stumble over the truth,
but most of them pick themselves up and
hurry off as if nothing ever happened.

—Winston Churchill

What you're about to read is intended to give you a roadmap for how to evaluate marketing communication. It's really that simple. No matter what the message, no matter who the audiences or conversationalists are, The 4Cs of Truth in Communications™ can help provide direction and guidance and ultimately help get you to your destination of effective communication. When I'm asked about the 4Cs of Truth in Communications, people expect to immediately get a simple recitation of the specific Cs. And ultimately, I get to that. But first I tell them why applying the *entire* model is important. At its core, the 4Cs model is an easily applied approach to identifying and validating stand-out, effective communication. Together, the 4Cs capture most everything that everyone connected with the project needs to know about consumer response to stimuli. Separately, they provide clarity—a simple way to categorize, analyze, and report on consumer response.

But before I get to divulge the Cs, I think it might make sense to explain how this process came about. The 4Cs methodology wasn't handed down from some mountaintop nor did it suddenly appear one day, fully formed like Venus on the half shell. On the contrary, this carefully structured approach had more humble origins. It started off almost ten years ago, as a way to present some focus group findings to an early strategic planning client, Helene Curtis.

Come to think of it, the 4Cs format was more a way for me to assemble the voluminous number of conversations I'd listened to across three different cities as consumers discussed the emotional threads that tie together the sense of self they associated with their hair. This was pretty heady stuff. And given that it was my first presentation to this client, I felt the need to deliver a cohesive and action-oriented presentation designed to clearly report the learning in a way with which everyone at the table, from client marketing, sales and senior management, to the agency creative people and the promotion agency, could jointly and readily identify. After all, nailing down what consumers are actually saying—and meaning—is not always an easy thing to do. And I thought it would be even more difficult to present this mother lode of information to such a disparate audience without some organization.

The pursuit of a tabla rasa

The first requirement of any genuinely useful research is a clean slate, which isn't always so easy to come by. Let's face it, all of us listen through filters of one sort or another. We all have predispositions and agendas. We all know our company's sacred cows. We all know our bosses' going-in assumptions. That's a lot of background noise to cut through. And the fact that most people aren't very good listeners in the first place doesn't help any. Careful, objective, really *true* listening, takes an enormous amount of effort and a willingness to "hear" things one may not want to hear.

Which helps explain why it's not the least bit uncommon to go into the back room of a focus group and discover that the ten people there are convinced they've heard five different and sometimes mutually exclusive things. Left to our own devices, most of us hear what we want or need to hear. And the rest of us aren't sure what exactly it is we're supposed to be listening for in the first place. This is precisely one of the things that makes my job so fascinating!

For example, if you've ever been in a consumer group session devoted to evaluating creative work—ads, packaging, whatever—to which the creative people responsible have been invited, I'm sure you've seen this phenomenon. I've worked in the front room and been an observer in the back room, and as an advocate for the creative folks, I can say this: it isn't fun to see your "babies" (what creative work is often likened to) be subjected to criticism, to be held up and sometimes unmercifully scrutinized. The backroom response is often, "Well, they just don't understand." Or almost as frequently, "They're too stupid to understand [my brilliance]." Which always reminds me of David Ogilvy's famous remark, "The consumer isn't a moron, she's your wife," (or husband as the case may be). My point, which I will be making throughout this book, is that sometimes the truth—whether it sounds stupid or not—can be difficult to hear. And so sometimes, the choice is made either not to hear it, or to hear a self-serving, bastardized version of it.

Over time it became obvious to me that what began as a clever technique for the presentation of focus group findings way back when, could actually be a rather objective tool to organize the way people listen and react to communication feedback. A way to supply the "eraser" necessary to get to a truly clean slate so people could listen objectively and actually learn something valuable. And that's what led me to an approach which might be likened to one first pioneered by the Boston Consulting Group (BCG).

Cow, dog, star or ?

More than three decades ago, this highly esteemed management consultant firm developed what it called a "matrix" for evaluating businesses or business units within a larger corporation. Using it, any operation could be deemed either a cash "cow" to be milked for immediate, bottom-line profits, a "dog" to be sold or closed down, a "star" to be invested in, or a "question mark," because no one was quite sure which it was yet. For those of us who were in graduate school in the mid-1980s, this matrix was the fundamental framework of many a case study.

Simple, yes. Almost to the point of being simplistic? Maybe. But it worked like a charm at helping people organize what might otherwise have been too much information, too many opinions, and a lot of frustratingly scattered thinking. Listening, I realized, could benefit from a similar corralling—thus the 4Cs, which we find not only help enormously in listening for the truth and in categorizing what we hear, but also leads to undeniably successful communication in the marketplace.

Comprehension, Connection, Credibility, and Contagiousness

Obviously, the value of the BCG matrix wasn't its scientific precision; it was just a supremely useful tool for organizing all this data—especially for those of us who visually process information. Likewise, there's nothing especially original about the 4C words you see here. However, used in combination, these words provide a remarkably holistic, easy to understand lexicon for evaluating and coming to grips with what is and isn't working in a piece of communication.

It's been my experience that the most useful concepts and applications are almost always simple, and this is a quantum leap beyond the vagaries of "they like it" or "it's just not doing anything for people." Even creative types have been known to readily accept the 4Cs model as an objective way to listen to how consumers evaluate their "babies."

Matching consumers' reactions to a piece of communications to a specific C—Comprehension, Connection, Credibility, or Contagiousness—provides a far more actionable set of data points. If people are getting the point but not believing the source, that is an addressable issue. If people are getting the message but not connecting with it on a personal, emotional level, that's something you can deal with. If everything is working except the message just isn't generating the excitement that leads to Contagiousness, that's worth knowing about. And of course, in using the 4Cs, the seamlessness and ease of discussing and organizing our thoughts on consumer feedback are glaringly apparent—especially when you've got multiple and disparate, but equally interested constituents involved.

From the bridge of the Titanic

Ultimately, the only value consumer research provides is to know what's out there in the dark while there's still time to do something about it—change course, stop, or maybe go full steam ahead. All of which can make the difference between steaming happily into port, possibly weeks ahead of schedule, or sharing a room with Charlie the Tuna.

Marketers need to know their consumers' "truth" so they can adjust their courses accordingly—before vast amounts of money (not to mention career trajectories) end up as literally "sunk" costs. And the 4Cs provide exactly that: *organized observations and prescriptive counsel that can be immediately acted upon*, either during the course of a multiple market study or through the ability to fix a rough cut or change a tagline, package copy, or visual. Time and again, I've been pleasantly surprised—and my clients have been even more delighted to see—how minor adjustments can have a major impact on the effectiveness of a piece of communications.

Maybe something we've all taken as a given, because we're so familiar with the brand or service, needs just a little more clarity to become fully comprehensible. Or maybe we need to dig a little deeper into the audience's world so we can establish a stronger, more visceral connection.

Painfully, but very much part of the truth, we may see that our consumption of the company Kool-Aid has blinded us to the fact that the folks out there just aren't buying it—even when we're fully convinced of it and saying it loudly with all our might.

And lastly, maybe what we're saying or the way we're saying it is fine, it's just nothing the audience is inclined to get terribly excited about. Any one or all of these discoveries presents the marketing communicator with the opportunity, dare I say, the *challenge*, to take his or her brand's message to the next level. And as you're about to see, this is what each C in the 4Cs is all about.

CHAPTER 1

The Truth Be Told

Truth is truth—to the end of reckoning.

—William Shakespeare
Measure for Measure: Act 5, Scene 1

I am a bad schmoozer. Bad at small talk too. Seriously. And given my 16 years in advertising agency account management, I'm sure that must have frustrated many a boss over the years. But schmoozing, to me, means hiding what you really want to say—otherwise known as the *truth*—behind thin veils of well-meaning platitudes and a few little white lies. Even the word itself, "schmooze," sounds a little slippery and artificial. But I've managed to get along in business—and more importantly in this life—pretty well as an anti-schmoozer. And those others of you out there like me know what I mean.

Speaking of small talk, it always irks me when someone starts off an answer to a question with, "Well, to be honest . . ." or, "Truthfully . . ." or, "If you want to know the truth . . ." Come to think of it, this is probably one of the reasons I am a bad schmoozer. These conversation starters always seem to emerge in a good "schmooze session." But when someone starts off that way, it usually leaves me wondering whether what he or she said to me prior to that caveat was at all genuine. Of course I want to know the truth!

I have a thing about the truth. Don't ask me why. It's just the way I am. This is part of the reason why I named my marketing consulting business Consumer Truth. I'm just at my best and most comfortable knowing that to the best of my ability, I am telling it like it is. Someone, a long time ago, once described me as "disgustingly honest." It was painful to hear at the time, but I've managed through the years and through self-acceptance and life experience, to put some positive spin on that. "Disgustingly honest" is simply being about truth.

As you can imagine, this is a predilection that did not always serve me so well when I was in account management at advertising agencies. I can't begin to count the number of times various bosses suggested to me that "things aren't always black and white," or that sometimes "you have to shade" or "sugar-coat" things. You can imagine how tough that was for me to swallow.

But they weren't entirely wrong. Things aren't always black and white (my husband will not believe these words are coming from me). However, I still think getting at the truth as best you can is incredibly important, and if you don't believe me, I have a far more authoritative source to back me up.

Jack Welch to the rescue

In his most recent book, *Winning*, this legendary CEO of General Electric goes on at some length about the supreme importance of what he calls "candor." After about 25 pages, I gave up counting the number of times he and his wife and co-author, Suzy Welch, used the word, but it would appear that they believe this is a critical—and often lacking—aspect of running a successful business.

As Mr. Welch tells it, he spent 20 years talking up the value of candor to various audiences at GE, but it was only after he retired that he realized how rare a commodity candor truly is. That its absence was, as he put it, "the biggest dirty little secret in business." His only explanation for this phenomenon is that from the time we're children, we're encouraged to soft peddle bad news and avoid confronting awkward truths. All of which he felt was a tremendous impediment to business success and one that could only be rectified by rewarding candor, praising it, and literally making heroes out of the people who practice it.

Why does Mr. Welch feel it necessary to hammer home this point so relentlessly? My guess is that it arose in response to the commonly held belief in business that "the numbers don't lie." Try telling that to the former shareholders of Enron or WorldCom.

The fact of the matter is, numbers can be spun to lie—to tell a nice story, in fact—and people will sometimes do almost anything to avoid telling the truth. Why else would the clichés "bitter truth" and "the truth hurts" exist? Not to mention the phrase, "don't shoot the messenger."

Candor is hard. In many quarters of business it is actively discouraged, as a boss once reminded me when she suggested that, "If you can't salute the man, at least salute the uniform," after I'd had a particularly rancorous, but entirely candid tussle with a higher-up.

I firmly believe the truth is essential not just to success, but often to survival. Just think for a second: What would have happened if someone had had the temerity to tell Hank Greenberg that some of the business tactics A.I.G. was employing were of dubious legality and could sink the company? The obvious answer is a definite pink slip. However, if Mr. Greenberg had actually listened, he might still have his own job.

And on an even bigger stage, what might have happened if anyone involved in John Kerry's 2004 campaign had told him, "John, you're brilliant, but you come across as an aloof, upper crust, intellectual snob that two-thirds of Americans can't relate to?" We might have been looking at a very different outcome.

However, when you play too fast and loose with the truth in business, you end up with things like Sarbanes-Oxley, or in politics, with campaign finance reform. Marketing has yet to receive that level of regulatory attention. In some ways that makes my job even harder.

"Divested" interests

The fundamental challenge to candor in the market research area is that by the time any approach or proposed solution arrives at our doorstep a tremendous amount of time and money has already gone into it. Many of the ideas have already been sold to top management. A lot of people have a vested interest in a particular outcome. They are looking for consumers to validate what each constituent already knows emphatically to be the "right" answer. The problem is there are often many constituents with many different "right" answers, and many of them are emphatic. In these situations, we have to fight the gravitational pull of all these agendas. One of the ways we do that is by remembering the New Coke disaster.

Legendary marketer and uber-consultant, Sergio Zyman, who was the CMO of Coca-Cola when this product was introduced, has made frequent reference to all the research that went into New Coke in several of the best-selling books he's written. And every time, he maintains that the problem was they never thought to ask people if discontinuing old Coke would matter to them. They did all the taste testing money could buy and probed every conceivable image dimension. They just forgot to ask this all-important behavioral question of the people who happened to really like Coke the way it was: What will you do if there's no more old Coke? The implication being that if they had asked that one simple question and the answer had come back, "Well, we'll rise up in rebellion," it would have meant, "stop the presses!" (or rather, the bottling machines) on New Coke.

But I'm not so sure. I've been in too many situations where people either heard what they wanted to hear or simply refused to accept what they were hearing. With all the technology invested in reformulating Coke, all the time spent persuading management, all the effort in winning over the bottlers and all the deep-rooted enmity toward its rival Pepsi, isn't it just as likely that the Coke peoples' reaction to the consumers' "rebellion" would have been total denial? I can just hear them saying, "It's too late, the train has left the station. We can't turn back now." And I can just as easily hear some market research person saying, "Well, okay, it's your nickel."

That's part of the trouble with this business of marketing consulting. It's often times far easier and more lucrative to figure out what clients want to hear as opposed to getting at the truth. When I was on the other side of the focus group mirror it was what always irritated me about consultants. I think it is undoubtedly how consultants get the rap of being people "who borrow your watch to tell you what time it is."

That's not how I operate. I don't borrow any of my clients' watches. But I do borrow something else from them.

The "consumer" part of Consumer Truth

I borrow my client's consumers. In fact, borrow is almost too gentle a term. I seize them and literally own them for the duration of the project. Of course, the client gets to help identify them—that's really the client's job, not mine. But once the particular demographic and psychographic parameters have been met, these people are mine. Mine to talk with, interrogate, explore, examine, and otherwise drill into for anything relevant to the client's issue at hand. And truthfully, I do.

What we're really looking for in any Truth Discovery Session (our own way of more accurately identifying what is traditionally called a focus group) is the consumer truth. Whether it's for brand positioning or new product development or communications evaluation, it's what we call "the consumer's closely held reality." That is, all those highly unpredictable, maddeningly idiosyncratic, but ever-so-firmly held beliefs and convictions that make up a particular consumer's or group of consumers' world view. That's what marketers desperately need to know if they ever hope to communicate with these people. That's the world view they need to speak to. Sometimes this is very difficult to do.

The consumers' truth isn't always the same as the marketer's truth. That might just be the understatement of the century. But which do you think matters most? Sometimes consumer truth makes no sense at all on the surface. Sometimes it seems totally inconsistent or illogical. It absolutely doesn't matter. Even when it seems like a well-reasoned argument could alter the consumers' truth, that's usually the steeper path to take. It's sailing into the wind, which any sailor knows, can be done. But a "tacking" course is always much, much longer, considerably slower, and requires much additional energy.

Knowing the consumers' truth—as painful and often surprising as it may be—is the equivalent of having the wind at your back, which is far more likely to produce smooth sailing (even in the wake of having to change course) and effective communication. And much like Jack Welch, we're obsessed with getting it for our clients. Does it sometimes hurt or frustrate them? I'm sure it does. Has it occasionally required total re-evaluation of painstakingly laid plans? It has. Does it sometimes mean that an advertising campaign or new package design may not hit the airwaves or shelf as soon as they'd like? Yes it does. But it sure beats the alternative: a failure to resonate with the very consumer for whom it is intended.

All of this might contribute to why Mr. Welch gives so much credit to candor as a primary catalyst to his myriad accomplishments at GE and why I'm feeling so strongly here about linking it to the truth. Truth, like candor, allows people to be themselves and to most optimally and transparently give their passion and energy in a way that invites those around them to take it all in, and perhaps even benefit from it. Telling it like it is might be why, as Mr. Welch explains it, ". . . each of us was better for it."

You gotta love that guy. I wonder if anyone ever referred to him as "disgustingly honest."

CHAPTER 2

A $500 Billion Missed Opportunity?

The truth is more important than the facts.

—Frank Lloyd Wright

It's become a cliché to say that we live in an "over-communicated" society. According to various sources, we are all exposed to anywhere from 1,000 to 3,000 commercial messages a day, supported by a worldwide advertising investment that McCann Universal's forecasting guru, Robert C. Coen, pegged at $575.1 billion in 2005. And that doesn't even include all the other communications we're exposed to on a daily basis—conversations, presentations, news, sports, weather, political debates, and the trillion e-mails we receive every day, at least half of which seem to be in your personal inbox at the moment.

But is this a case of "over-communication," or is it something else? Personally, I'm inclined to believe the latter. I think it would be much more accurate to say we are "over-messaged" rather than "over-communicated." The vast majority of these messages go flying right past us. And that's a huge issue. Faced with the challenge of producing earnings that are real, not manufactured, confronted by the limitations of regulatory scrutiny, corporations—and especially their marketing people—are beginning to realize that it's not enough to just "get your message out there." Today a message has to truly *communicate* with people. It has to attract their attention, make sense to them, connect with them on a personal level, be believable, and ideally, be worth getting excited about. As the dramatic increase in internet keyword advertising demonstrates—with Google's advertising doubling in just the last year to $6.1 billion —John Wanamaker's "Half my advertising is wasted, the trouble is I don't know which half" adage just doesn't cut it anymore. In fact, to be more precise on that fraction, the cover article in the August 7, 2006 issue of *Advertising Age* reports a key finding of market research veteran Rex Briggs' soon-to-be-released book, *What Sticks: Why Most Advertising Fails and How to Guarantee Yours Succeeds.* He reportedly clarifies with statistical certainty that it's actually only 37.3 percent of marketers' advertising budgets that are wasted. Whew! That must be quite a relief to those packaged goods and automobile advertisers who spend tens or hundreds of millions of dollars on advertising each year. I'd guess it is also quite a wake up call to ad agencies, whose accountability bar for that other 62.7 percent is likely to become a bit higher.

It might well be this groundswell of an accountability movement that has driven the growth of our business, Consumer Truth. That's because we've developed an astonishingly powerful process—the 4Cs of Truth in Communications—for objectively evaluating whether a piece of communication is genuinely *communicating.* In other words, is it saying what you think it's saying? Does anyone who is hearing it care? And if not, why is that and what can you, the "communicator," do about it?

But before we get to that, let's spend a little time exploring why communicating appears to be so hard. Most of us know how to talk by the age of two; you'd think we'd be pretty effective communicators by the time we're twenty or forty years older.

If a tree falls in the forest . . .

You know this old thought puzzle: ". . . and there's no one there to hear it, does it make a sound?" I long ago gave up trying to figure that one out, but I've always thought there was a scary analog to this conundrum in the traditional advertising paradigm.

In this case, the way it goes is: "As long as we *know* there are people in the forest, can't we be *sure* that the falling tree (our message) will be heard?" Heard? Maybe. But paid attention to? That's a different story. Have an *impact?* An entirely different genre. And that's what the 4Cs are all about—helping communicators find something to say and a meaningful way to say it that will really *matter* to and excite their audience. When you have that *Connection*, attention is sure to follow, but it's getting harder all the time. In fact, in a fascinating book that came out in 2001, *The Attention Economy*, authors Thomas H. Davenport and John C. Beck made the statement, "In postindustrial societies, *attention* (emphasis mine) has become a more valuable currency than the kind you store in bank accounts."

The marketing communications business has responded to this reality in two ways. First, it has wildly embraced the internet keyword search model, reasoning quite sensibly that if a person is "Googling" a word relevant to your brand, surely that person is interested and will pay attention to your message. However, that short little text ad is hardly going to build a long-term, emotional relationship with a brand. So, secondly, marketers continue to resort to what I've heard described as advertising's "insanity defense," repeating the same activity over and over again in anticipation of different results.

For example, take the Verizon guy who's been asking us for what seems like a hundred years, "Can you hear me now?" Can you remember when you first started noticing this communication? Can you remember when you first connected it with the brand Verizon? How did you feel about Verizon then, and how about now? And perhaps most tellingly, are you a Verizon customer today and would you be tomorrow, if a better offer came along? Casual inquiries would lead me to believe, no. Despite the fact that Verizon spent hundreds of millions of dollars on communicating this message in 2005 and similar amounts in prior years, and despite the fact that the tagline has achieved every marketer's dream of actually becoming part of the consumer lexicon, I wonder if Verizon is still struggling to truly connect with its audience. I'd venture to say it might be a lot more economically efficient for Verizon to successfully communicate to its audience the message that Verizon's superior network is all that really matters when you want to get and keep a mobile phone connection. The beat-it-into-them communications strategy only works if you have a billion dollars to throw at it, year after year. But why throw a billion dollars of the shareholders' money at "messaging" people every year, if you can *communicate* with them for a fraction of that amount?

The "John Hancock" moment

We all know there's a better way of going about it because we can all cite examples of occasions when a piece of advertising genuinely engaged us on first exposure, not the fiftieth or five hundredth time we saw it. These are ads that really communicated with us, and when an ad or any other sort of message, from an inspiring sermon to a rousing political speech, truly communicates with us, the effect is almost instantaneous and often has far-reaching and lasting effects. There's no lag time or slow build, you can almost remember where you were and what you were doing when you first saw or heard the message.

I like to call these "John Hancock" moments because one memorable experience with this phenomena was when I saw the John Hancock "real life, real answers" advertising campaign for the first time. I can remember where I was (the kitchen table) and what I was doing (watching the morning news and having a cup of coffee), when the spot came on. And I can still remember what it was about—a father holding his baby daughter and discussing the realities of their financial future. I didn't need to see this commercial multiple times to get it or relate to it. Once was enough, and this was despite the fact that at the time I had no husband, let alone children, and my financial future was largely entrusted to the vast array of New York City restaurants and increasingly escalating New York City rents.

The John Hancock spot simply "spoke" to me. Plainly and simply, it communicated. It was a very fresh approach, so it got my attention. Its message was clear. It made a powerful emotional connection with me. I knew enough about John Hancock's reputation to believe it. And it was riveting enough to stop me in my tracks on one exposure. It's tempting to add that this spot and the campaign it was a part of went on to win a lot of advertising industry awards. But there's a better coda to the story. This advertising campaign was a key component of the company's new CEO, David D'Alessandro's, effort to reinvigorate the John Hancock brand. He accomplished it so successfully that a few years later he was able to sell the company to the Canadian insurance firm, Manulife, for $10.9 billion, or a nearly 20 percent premium to its stock price at the time.

But this is just one example. If we try, we can all rattle off dozens of instances where communication that really connected with people, or really *communicated* with them, had a profound effect on the fortunes of those involved. Apple would in all likelihood not have survived long enough to invent iTunes and the iPod were it not for the extraordinary loyalty it engendered with its audience largely through consistently effective communications. One need only look at Gateway to see what becomes of a small-share computer maker that hasn't taken advantage of this tool. Altoids started off with a communications budget of less than a million dollars a year and in half a decade was able to grow its sales from less than $20 million a year to over $120 million a year. What Altoids said to people, and probably more importantly in this case, the *way* it said it to them, really mattered to its audience. So its message truly *communicated.* Anyone attempting to do the same should not be satisfied with less. But how the heck do you do it?

Out of the mouths of babes

The bulk of this book will be devoted to looking at specific aspects of communication and discussing what works, what doesn't, and why. But first, there are some overarching principles that need to be addressed, starting with what we know about how the human brain processes information.

There's been enough work done on a scientifically rigorous, experimental basis to assert that human beings are unrepentant novelty freaks, commencing from a very young age. Seriously, so many studies have demonstrated that very young babies quickly tire of looking at the same object and turn away, only to be galvanized by something new. There's a reason that the word "new" ranks right up there with "free" for its ability to capture attention. And this has also been borne out in our investigation of the fourth C, Contagiousness, which we'll elaborate on later. Suffice it to say for now, we've observed that the correlation between the novelty of a message's content and approach is virtually 1.0 with its Contagiousness factor. People just seem to be hard-wired to love the novel and are unable to stop themselves from wanting to share the "news."

The other element brain researchers have provided us with is incontrovertible evidence that every form of stimuli that enters our brain—sights, sounds, commercials, package design, or political stump speeches—elicits a visceral, emotional reaction long before it produces a rational one. This is the famous "snake-stick" experience some of us have experienced at least once in our lives while walking through the woods. You glance down and see a shape that looks enough like a snake that you almost leap straight into the air, heart pounding on adrenaline, only to realize nano-seconds later, it's just a stupid stick. The survival instinct of this over-reaction is easy to understand, but it's much harder for some of those more right-brain challenged people to accept this reality. They would be much more comfortable if the world proceeded on an entirely rational, logical basis.

So given these two overarching principles, what's a marketer to do? Marketing authority Seth Godin's advice in his book, *Purple Cow*, is to make everything you do exceptional. It's nice on paper, but a little impractical in the everyday world. You can make your communications exceptional and that's a good start. However, that means you're going to have to begin thinking about *how* you communicate things and not just *what* it is you're trying to communicate.

A rose by any other name might not sound as sweet

What you have to say and how you go about saying it are two entirely different things, as this amusing parlor game demonstrates. Just take any famous quote and rephrase it in plain English.

Thomas Paine's famous quote, "These are the times that try men's souls," suddenly becomes: The situation is very bad right now. Franklin Delano Roosevelt's "The only thing we have to fear is fear itself," might come out as: This is no time to lose our heads. And Will Rogers's immortal phrase, "The only difference between death and taxes is that death doesn't get worse every time Congress meets," would be rendered as: The only thing they do in Washington is raise our taxes.

Not quite the same are they? That's simply because the novelty of the expression and thus an enormous amount of its emotional resonance has been drained away. Or as Mark Twain once said, "The difference between the right word and the almost right word is the difference between lightning and a lightning bug."

So I can imagine some of you throwing your hands in the air and saying, "Oh, great, so now she's suggesting our marketing communications should sound like they were written by Will Rogers, or our candidate's speeches need to sound like FDR? What next, our packaging should look like it was designed by Paul Rand?"

Well, why not? Why not aspire to those heights? I never said creating communication that really communicates was going to be easy. But you know that parlor game we were just playing? It also works very nicely in the realm of marketing communications. Just take any famous advertising tagline you can think of and restate it in plain English:

When it absolutely, positively has to be there overnight, might be rendered as, "When it's important, we'll get it there tomorrow."

The ultimate driving machine, would become, "A very well-engineered car."

And one of the most famous advertising taglines of all times, *Just do it*, might have been, "Get off your a—." (Although come to think of it, that might have worked, too.)

As you can see, with the novelty of expression stripped away, it loses a lot. That's really what we at Consumer Truth spend a lot of our time doing—deconstructing our client's communications efforts, determining if they are firing on all cylinders and if not, how they can or what's missing.

But sometimes, the reason a message isn't coming through with the force its creators desire isn't just a matter of uninspired phrasing. Sometimes it signals a more delicate and difficult problem.

What lies beneath

Given this is our primary means of gathering the strategic insight with which we help marketers better communicate their brands' positioning, it is obviously not my intention to denigrate the focus group. Conducted well, I firmly believe in the power and insight derived by getting under the skin of consumers. We've spent literally hundreds of hours talking to consumers in a group setting to discover brand and positioning "truths" which inform our positioning communications recommendations. But we don't do it in the same way as the groups I observed when I used to sit on the other side of the mirror.

That's really one of the underlying principles of the whole 4Cs process. I was concerned that somehow conventional focus groups weren't always getting to the essence of things, the true crux of the matter. They were spending a lot of time scratching the surface or digging for what I always thought to be rather surface analogies. Do you like this? Why or why not? If this product was an animal, what would it be? What kind of car would it drive? Obviously, there's considerable evidence of this surface scratching since virtually every significant piece of communication out there, from advertising to car designs to packaging to political campaigns, has been focus-grouped like crazy, and in some unfortunate cases, to death! If much of this "communicating" isn't being heard, there must be something wrong with the process.

Fixing it wasn't easy. It took me several years to develop and refine all the techniques necessary to fully deliver the promise of the 4Cs of Truth in Communications. However, along the way, I discovered there's another major impediment to creating communication that people genuinely hear and embrace.

There's no better way to describe it than to ask you to recall the riveting movie, *A Few Good Men*. Do you remember the penultimate scene in this courtroom drama where Tom Cruise has finally backed Jack Nicholson, the Colonel Jessup character, into a corner? And Jessup completely loses it and bellows to the entire, stunned courtroom, "You want the truth?! You *can't handle* the truth!" Without question, this is a definite eyes-glued-to-the-screen moment.

Yes, that's what I discovered was the biggest problem of all. Many marketers, many business people, many political candidates and their consultants, many "people-people," when you come right down to it, view the truth more or less the same way Superman viewed kryptonite. They just can't handle it. We'll get into this more in the next chapter, but since we touched on brain research a short time ago, I wanted to share this last factoid from that area of academia.

Thanks to the research that's been done, and perhaps even more thanks to the geniuses who invented the functional magnetic resonance imaging (MRI) technology, which allows scientists to observe the human brain in action as it responds to various stimuli, it is now believed that human beings are actually phenomenal B.S. detectors, but not on a conscious level; it happens on an instinctive, gut level.

One theory that's been put forth to explain this, which I find somewhat fascinating, is based on the observation that human beings are dependent upon each other and have been for thousands of years. In fact, the theorists speculate that this was the case for our ancestors long before sophisticated language skills had evolved. We had to *know* if our co-clan members or co-cave mates were cheating because our very survival depended on everyone pulling his or her own weight. So theorists wonder if we evolved super-sophisticated, gut instincts for when the truth is being communicated and when it's not, simply to survive.

If that were the case, it would go miles toward explaining why so many methods of evaluating communications miss the mark. They are too rational, too logical, too based on asking people what they think instead of really getting at what they *feel*—what matters to them, what motivates them, and importantly, what de-motivates them? This is the core of my approach. And I think it would be easy to make the case that if the message that someone is trying to communicate rings fundamentally un-true to the target, he or she is not only contributing to that $500 billion dollar communications sinkhole, he or she is also flying in the face of fifty thousand years of human evolution.

CHAPTER 3

The First C: Comprehension— Get it? Got it? Good.

You Just Don't Understand

—Deborah Tannen

.

Given the extraordinary amount of thought and planning that goes into the development of any professional communication, from advertising to a TV pilot to a political "stump" speech, you would think simply understanding the message would never be a problem. But just as Ms. Tannen discovered in studying the difficulties men and women have communicating with each other, it's not that easy. Sometimes people just don't "get it." The intended message a marketer thinks is so clear, or the point a candidate is trying so hard to make, somehow gets lost in the telling.

The Comprehension C is exactly what you think it is— there's no hidden meaning or great deal of explanation necessary, although it is obviously quite fundamental to basic communication. It is, quite simply, do they *get it?* Does the audience get the message, the main idea, the point? Is the audience able to internalize the message such that they can play it back? This confirms that they get it. It also confirms the message has penetrated. If they don't get it, it's not getting through. And if it's not getting through, your time, energy, and efforts are wasted, as are theirs. Because even if they like the message or can relate to it, if it's not what you wanted them to hear/read/see/feel, it really doesn't matter. In fact, it's a different message altogether, which could have potentially severe adverse effects.

Let's take an example. The Home Depot, venerated founder of the consumer-friendly home improvement business had always been the leader in this category. But about five or six years ago, Lowe's Home Improvement Centers began to encroach on their turf and The Home Depot found its hold on the category loosening up a bit. It needed to re-establish its King Kong-like grip on the category of home improvement, and it landed on a benefit area encapsulated by the tagline, "*You can do it. We can help.*" I think that's about as clear as you can get in the area of message communication. To me, it says so much—"You, Mr. or Mrs. Homeowner, have the ability to be the master of your home repair domain. You can fix that sink or tile that bathroom floor yourself. We (Home Depot) are a home improvement store that you've known and have been familiar with for many years. We are here to support you in your efforts to fix up your home yourself. We empower you with the ability to do it right." To take it to a personal level, I—Mrs. Homeowner—know very clearly what they are communicating to me. I get it. Next.

Let's take a different one. My husband Ken and I were driving on the expressway recently and we saw this billboard image of a woman's hand whose ring finger bore an enormous diamond and was extended out while the other three fingers and thumb were closed. From a distance it looked like one big flip off. So it was visually arresting, no doubt. It definitely got my attention. As we got closer, I saw the copy, and since I happened to be the passenger, I could take the time to read it (Ken, on the other hand, just got the "flip off" message). *This woman is not enraged, she's engaged.* What's the message? What did they want me to know about that diamond? And who are "they"? Frankly, I can't tell you. I didn't even notice whether it was a diamond brand or a jewelry store. I just saw the image, read the copy, and then rolled my eyes.

Please don't make me work that hard. I am very busy.

From my very early days as an assistant account executive working at Ted Bates Advertising in New York, I have constantly wondered why marketers and advertisers want consumers to work so hard to figure out the basic message. And what makes them think consumers have the time or inclination to do so? After conducting more than 1,000 group or individual interviews, in-homes ethnographies and on-site interviews over many years, talking to something like 5,000 consumers, I can say unequivocally that consumers just don't have the time or interest to sit there and figure out what it is you're *trying* to say to them. In a recent round of Truth Discovery Sessions my partner Ken conducted with corporate professionals (and these are people who are supposed to be a little higher up on the evolutionary scale of message comprehension) for a corporate conglomerate holding company, the Comprehension C was dismally evasive. The corporate professionals repeatedly told him, "I'm just not going to spend that much time figuring out what they're trying to say to me. I'm already turning the page." I can definitely corroborate that from your everyday-Joe consumer perspective as well. Consumers are busy. There's a lot going on in their lives. We hear that no matter what category we're delving into, from ice cream to electronics to coffee, shampoo, cereal, or insurance. People are busy, busy, busy. Generally, they're perfectly willing to listen to your message. In fact, many *want* to hear it. They just don't want to work *hard* to get it.

Now, getting back to that "flip off" ring ad—talk about bad placement. Not two minutes down the road on the opposite side, there was an ad for Cartier diamond rings (did you notice that I *got* the brand message right away?). All I remember is three heart-shaped diamond rings elegantly clustered together and the brand name. What's the message I got? Cartier designs really nice diamond rings. And short of sounding off on marketing strategy for outdoor ads, when you're communicating in a medium where your target is driving by at 60 miles an hour, the message needs to be just that simple. In this very simple case, it's clear which message I got, and which convoluted message I didn't get. And I wasn't even driving. Comprehension of a message is very important, a key variable to understanding what we call The Big Truths™ in communication—those topline, gut reactions consumers have to what marketers are saying to them. Take note: they are not easily revised.

So how can you tell if the target gets it? Well, it's simple. If they get it, they can tell you. Quite easily, as a matter of fact. They can internalize the message and play it back to you in their own words, just as I did with the Cartier diamond ad and the Home Depot message. Internalizing the message confirms not only that they *get it,* but that it has penetrated. Keep in mind this has nothing to do with whether or not they like it or agree with it—or in any way, shape, or form, how they feel about it. I haven't discussed whether or not I connected with The Home Depot or the Cartier messages, whether I was motivated by them or interested in them. But what's important at the outset is just about *getting it.* The Comprehension C simply evaluates whether or not what you intended to communicate remotely resembles what your audience heard/saw/read/felt.

The first "cut" is the deepest

So when we talk to consumers about a piece of stimulus—whether it's a finished ad, a storyboard, a verbal concept, a website design, or a logo or package design, after gleaning their "gut" reaction, the first thing we ask them is, "What did this communicate to you or tell you about, specifically? What's the main message?" and we evaluate right away whether or not it reflects the intended message. This is the closest reflection of real-world reception of the message. It's that first "cut" that matters most. And this can be applied to other forms of communication as well—think about a speech, a movie "treatment," a class syllabus, a manuscript for a book, a report, a newspaper or magazine article—whatever is being communicated by whatever means employed, needs to be fully comprehended to even begin to break through. What does the message instantly communicate? And so, it is important that Comprehension gets nailed down first. If the intended message is not being communicated, we have a problem. And we need to understand what's driving that before we can move on to the other three Cs. Pretty simple, right? Comprehension is a pretty fundamental communication truth. Got it.

So what are some ways you can be sure if your target—no matter the communication vehicle—*gets it?* You can start by making sure the message is clear and sharp. If so, it is likely to penetrate. And I'm still not talking about relevance, likability, or meaningfulness of the message. I'm just saying that, typically, if it's clear—the target completely understands it without having to decipher anything or dig out any hidden meanings—and sharp—the message "cuts" instantly and the target inherently *knows* what you mean—it will penetrate. Whether you have 15 seconds or two hours, a column or the next *War and Peace*, if the message is not clear and sharp, it's likely not going to be understood. But, failing clarity and pierce-ability, repetition can sometimes help. This would support the long-held "rules" for a great presentation:

1. Tell them what you're going to tell them.

2. Tell them.

3. Tell them what you told them.

We often find that when a main benefit is communicated several times through the message, whether it's in an emotional or rational way, consumers tend to get it better by the end of the exposure.

But don't go too deep

In the marketing community, I sometimes find it amazing how positioning statements that people have spent months "wordsmithing" can confound the heck out of an audience that's otherwise completely familiar with the topic. And sometimes messages that are grounded in a "higher order" benefit go completely over peoples' heads. I was watching one-on-one interviews in Atlanta very early in my advertising agency account management career, where a trained psychologist was hired to find out the deep, emotionally-laden, untapped, and underlying reasons why consumers chewed gum (and these are adults we're talking about). Yes, you read that correctly. *Gum.* Two and a half hours of being asked "WHY?" and "HOW?" relative to every conceivable attribute and benefit of gum-chewing. Here's a little taste of how the interview generally transpired:

Respondent: *I chew gum because I like the taste.*
Interviewer: WHY do you like the taste?
R: *Because it tastes good.*
I: WHY does it taste good?
R: *Because I like the taste of spearmint.*
I: WHY do you like the taste of spearmint?
R: ***Because it tastes good!***
I: WHY is it important that it tastes good?
R: *What?*

R: *I chew gum because it gives me something to do.*
I: HOW does it give you something to do?

R: *It helps me concentrate.*

I: HOW does it help you concentrate?

R: *Because it gives me something to focus on.*

I: HOW does it give you something to focus on?

R: **Because it gives me something to do!**

I: WHY is it important that you have something to do?

R: *What?*

R: *I chew gum because it gets rid of my bad breath.*

I: HOW does it get rid of your bad breath?

R: *It has a minty taste that makes my breath smell like mint.*

I: WHY is it important to get rid of your bad breath?

R: *What?*

So after this line of questioning continued for a couple of hours, one patient, gracious, and very polite woman leaned in close to the psychologist/interviewer and said in a quintessential southern accent, "Honey, what ARE you gettin' at? Gum is gum!" This phrase subsequently became the mantra of both the agency and the client for years after. Yes, consumers say the darndest things! I love them all (well, *most* of them). Of course, gum is gum! And it's difficult for consumers to internalize a message about a product or service that is incongruous with their own experience. Looking back, it's hard for me to personally imagine two and a half hours in a one-on-one session in a dark room talking about any product, service, or condition with a consumer—even one that is a little higher on the involvement meter—let alone gum! Which probably explains why "*keep it simple, stupid,*" is a mantra of political and marketing consultants everywhere. Sometimes consumers get all they need to or are capable of getting, and you don't want or need to push it beyond that.

Yet even when a message is clear as a bell and consumers understand the message, sometimes they still don't seem to truly *get it*. How can that be? Possibly because the message isn't saying anything that *matters* to them. And if a message doesn't connect with its audience on a personal level, it can wind up effectively ineffective. Let's take a look at the next C.

CHAPTER 4

The Second C: Connection

Yeah, baby!

—Austin Powers, International Man of Mystery

Making connections is what we spend our everyday lives doing. We've been doing it since we were kids. Connecting the dots; putting the round pegs in the round holes; going from Point A to Point B in a story problem; getting the bat on the ball for a solid hit. There's something innately clarifying and gratifying about making connections. Something has been accomplished. Something has been achieved. When a plug gets inserted into an electrical socket, there is light and energy; things turn on; they *go*. Making a Connection with a communicated idea or message means not only that the audience *gets it*, but that it resonates with them. It strikes an intuitive chord. It has, somehow, innate meaning and significance to them.

Messages and ideas that make rational connections are on their way to truly meaning something to the audience, and more importantly, to sparking new behaviors and actions. From where we sit, there is nothing more exciting than when we see a piece of communication truly *connect* on all levels with its audience. It really is a powerful moment, almost a Sally Field "They really like me!" moment, or to date myself less, a Halle Barry "she-just-couldn't-believe-she-won-an-Oscar" moment, and was rendered temporarily mute. It's the moment when it becomes impossible to ignore that the message has made a visceral Connection with the audience. It's that "yes!" feeling. A genuine rapport has been established. It's no longer advertiser talking to customer, or politician to voter; it's a message from someone who really knows me and *understands what matters to me.* So much so, that I feel that the message is speaking directly to me on a personal level. "My message, my friend. Yes!"

Connecting with the consumer means you have begun to establish a relationship with them via your brand's communication. And how valuable is that?! It means something you said or showed to them has reached them on some internal level, whether it's in a rational or irrational way, and so the communication [the message] resonates too. The message somehow has tapped into an existing consumer truth for them in their lives relative to the subject. It usually reaches down to something emotional, or at the very least, something that is not entirely rational: frustration, excitement, anger, passion, joy, happiness, sadness, resignation, etc. We've found that the branding part comes in if the consumer/audience is able to take your brand's message to that innate, intuitive place. They can relate to the brand better because they have made a Connection with the message. It's relatively simple to pinpoint a rational Connection. Consumers will tell you "I can relate to that because . . ." Their answer will give some clues or insights as to why there may be an emotional Connection buried in there that is worth probing.

I can see myself!

Here's an example that serves to demonstrate how the Connection C completely takes over when it's right on the money. I was working on a communications evaluation project for a new Suave® hair care campaign—at the time, a completely new message based on a new positioning and tapping into a newly discovered consumer truth. Three print ads depicted "mom" (the target) in various family life situations: (See Figures 4.1, 4.2, and 4.3)

It's possible to have perfectly obedient curls without having to repeat yourself fourteen times.

Say yes to beautiful without paying the price.

© Unilever Corp.

FIGURE 4.1   Mom in the kitchen multi-tasking by making a PB&J sandwich while having a phone conversation—with her kids all around her doing various real-life, kid-type things.

The tagline reads: *Say yes to beautiful without paying the price.*

FIGURE 4.2   Mom in the bathroom literally sitting on a (closed) commode and helping her toddler with potty training while her 4-year-old is brushing his teeth.

FIGURE 4.3   Mom in the hallway helping her young daughter get her shoes on with her sons playing in the background.

All real-life situations to be sure. If you held a mirror up to a mom they are likely to say, "I can see myself!" So what? That doesn't necessarily mean she likes what she sees, is moved emotionally, or is otherwise motivated by that image. But in this case, it did mean that. One mom looked at those three ads and said, literally, as she pointed to each one of them, "That's me, that's me, and that's me!" The Connection wasn't made simply because she could see herself in those situations—and here's the interesting, brand-relevant part—it was made because she connected with a life truth communicated by each of the headlines *and* because she saw that each of the moms depicted ("me, me, me") *had great looking hair.* And she was able to connect with the message that "even though I'm a mom and have a crazy, chaotic mom life, using Suave can help me look good!" The beautiful epilogue to this story is that in subsequent quantitative ad testing, these ads met all client hurdles for Attention, Branding, Communication, and Motivation. And the Suave® hair care brand has begun to experience share and sales growth. As a consumer insight consultant to a great, long-time client, a consumer truth and insight-seeker, and fellow mom, I'll just add, "yeah, baby!"

Solve the <u>right</u> problem. Make the Connection.

Another way to tell whether your message or your communication has made a connection with consumers is if they immediately begin to "fit" the product or message into their everyday lives. They actually can visualize it there in experiences that they've had or that they might have. That's a powerful message, because there's no need to spend any time or effort to persuade your audience any further. They already *know* how to relate to this message. They can visualize it. They're perked up. "Yes! I can see that."

We did some work a while ago with some frozen dessert products, exploring many different potential benefit areas spanning from functional to emotional. What we found was that no matter what unique benefit we offered up to consumers in whatever innovative manner, the benefit that mattered most in this segment was taste. No matter how we tried to move them off the taste platform, no matter how far out we went, taste is where they invariably returned every time—like a boomerang. It's the only thing that made sense. Nothing else could even come close to be being relevant. Of course, thinking about frozen desserts, it all does make sense, doesn't it? It's got to be about the pure sensory enjoyment, or why bother?

But all was not lost. We did find a resonant benefit beyond taste; it just happened not to apply to this product. Without any stimulus from us, consumers translated what was an irrelevant non-taste-focused benefit for frozen desserts targeted to adults into a completely relevant functional benefit for frozen hand-held novelties targeted to kids. These mothers or grandmothers of young children could immediately envision how one small segment of their lives would be just a little bit better if they could give their kids ice pops, ice cream bars, and cones without having to worry. Now we've made a connection. This was something that truly mattered to them. A problem (albeit small in the scheme of things) they had experienced in the past and knew they would continue to experience in the future could potentially be solved forever. Suddenly it all just completely clicks. *Yeah, baby!*

Is there such a thing as too much of a Connection?

Along with many other consumer insight consultants, I worked on the beginning stages of that now famous Dove® "Campaign for Real Beauty" that uses real women instead of beautiful models to communicate benefits about their hair and skin products. I worked on the hair part of this huge and ultimately groundbreaking effort for women. You've seen the billboards. You've seen the women on Oprah. You've read the reviews. You know the campaign. Talk about *Contagiousness*—which as I'll explain later, is almost always linked to Connection. And if you're a regular woman, you can totally relate to the message those ads put out. I can tell you from my early work on hair, the message was positively empowering and inspiring. Women loved this message. Yes! It's about time some beauty brand came out and addressed the real looking women like me who use its products. My hair is not necessarily blonde, stick-straight and silky, but I am beautiful too. Thank you, Dove,® for understanding that about me and speaking to me in that way. Women loved the message, they totally got it, and connected with it quickly and unequivocally. And they gave Dove® all the proper credit for blazing a trail in their marketing efforts, for being unafraid to address real women in real ways.

There may have been just one slight problem along the way. They were so caught up in the consumer truth, so caught up in totally connecting with the message that they almost forgot about the hair benefits. Kind of an interesting problem. Your target absolutely connects with your message, they "brand" the message to your particular brand, but the message is so strong and emotionally powerful that it obscures the brand's communication of functional benefits. Now what? Well, I'd say in this case, the hit was of such huge magnitude, so visually and emotionally arresting, so well-branded to Dove,® and so darned *contagious* and ground-breaking, that the overall brand wins, even if specific, lower-rung hair benefits are temporarily overwhelmed. But I definitely am a bit biased! On a more objective note, the brand's share of market—the ultimate arbiter of marketing success—has increased over the past two years. So, back to my sub-head question above—is there such a thing as making too much of a Connection? What do you think?

By this time, I think you've seen that making a Connection with a communicated idea or message not only means the audience *gets* the message, but it resonates with them on a personal level. It strikes a chord. It is something they can intuitively relate to because it has innate and personal meaning for them. There is light and energy. Things turn on. They *go*. Providing, of course, that the message is believable, which takes us to the next chapter.

CHAPTER 5

The Third C: Credibility

Not a trace of doubt in my mind.

—Davey Jones, "I'm a Believer"

To be persuasive we must be believable; to be believable we must be credible; to be credible we must be truthful.

—Edward R. Murrow

Okay, they may *get* the message; they may *connect* with the message and it may be relevant to their lives. But if the message isn't credible, if it doesn't conform to its brand's (or cause's, or platform's) truth, it's meaningless. The audience needs to believe *who* is saying it (e.g. the brand's voice), *what* is being said, and *how* it is being said. Otherwise any Connection previously established immediately begins to break down. And I mean *immediately*.

- *Who?* Does it make sense for your brand to speak to its audience in this way? Does it logically fit, given the equity your brand has developed among its core target and in the marketplace as a whole, that this message is delivered in this particular way?

- **What?** Is it something your audience expects from this brand? This could be good and bad. It could be good because if it fits expectations, it is unquestioned. There's an immediate head-nod; the target is already moving on to other aspects of the message, like Comprehension or Connection. *And,* if it's something expected, it could likely get glossed over or even ignored outright. It may fit, but if it's just "same-old," there better be enough going on in the areas of Communication and Connection (and Contagiousness, the fourth C) to make up for too smooth a fit.

- **How?** An unexpected message or delivery can bring a lot of energy and attention to your brand, especially if its history or heritage or equity give it permission to speak in this way. Or even if it doesn't, it can still be powerful if marketplace conditions and consumer attitudes make it acceptable anyway.

The point is, to twist around the Edward R. Murrow quote above:

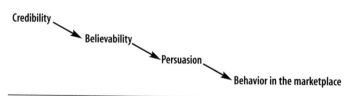

Credibility → Believability → Persuasion → Behavior in the marketplace

So even if it's not *instantly* credible, it becomes credible because your audience can see a way to make the message fit. That counts too. You can imagine that this is the

C some clients have told us gets 100 percent for pain. But we didn't name our company Consumer *Truth* just as a branding device; we meant it. Because let's face it, every company, every organization, every team has its Kool-Aid, and there's nothing wrong with that. It's part of what holds organizations together. The only problem comes when you invite new guests to the party through your communications, invite them to sample your Kool-Aid, and they unceremoniously spit it out on the floor. Yuck!

Reebok spent nearly two decades trying to be Nike only to ultimately give up and agree to be acquired by Adidas. Coca-Cola has probably spent well over a billion dollars over the ages trying to be as youthful and cool as Pepsi. However, at their very essence, brands are generally what they are. They are, inevitably, where they have been embedded and "placed" by their consumers. Brands have truths, too. And this is part of what Consumer Truth helps its clients discover. Brands can stretch up to a point, but beyond that (unless there are hundreds of millions of dollars lying around), it may be a hopeless undertaking.

Discover your brand's truth

In almost every positioning study we do for any client, we always include an exercise called Brand Truth Discovery. This is another method we've developed to quickly determine where the brand, and equally as important, its competitors, sit in consumers' psyches. It's rational on the surface, but what comes out is undoubtedly rooted in emotional soil. We find out through a series of bi-polar associations:

- *What the brand is and what it is not.* That tells us right away what the "edges" of the brand are within the category, and the limits of consumer acceptance. It also provides a kind of roadmap for where the brand can credibly be taken. Of course, my Target example in the following pages will serve to illustrate that with a ton of mass media support and consistently brilliant creative and on-site follow-through, even the edges of consumer acceptance can be breached!

- *What it stands for and what it stands against in the minds of consumers.* This begins to get at emotional connections, underpinnings of loyalty and longstanding beliefs and their origins. This touches on a brand's iconic status, potential toward iconic status, or lack thereof.

- *What it is an expert in and what it knows nothing about.* This tells us the true brand equity as well as inherent lack of Credibility. It also begins to get at brand differentiation and elements of ownability.

The polarities go on and on, and we customize them by category, client, and of course, the real brand truths emerge in our in-depth analysis. But when we know all these juicy brand attachments for our brand as well as its competitors, well, you can just imagine the maps that we as marketing consultants begin to create with this insight. Fabulous! Brand positioning opportunities that emerge straight from consumer perception, right off the top of their heads, discovered in about 15 to 20 minutes. Imagine that!

The Credibility C is all about your brand's truth. It's either going to work for consumers or it isn't, because of the attachments made. For a message to be really driving the Credibility train means it makes sense for your brand's message to be communicated in that particular way. It gets an immediate head-nod. No question about it. Not a trace of doubt in their minds. When Credibility is there, it removes a potential obstacle to Comprehension, Connection, and Contagiousness. In fact, when it's instantly credible, consumers don't even think about it. They don't usually look at an ad or package or concept which is delivering a credible brand message and say, "Yes, that is a believable message from that brand." In most of the work we do, Credibility of the message is not an issue. Most clients know their own brand's truth—it's the fiber of their brand. It's been built up and ingrained in consumers' brains and psyches over time. It's been evident in the way they make brand choices. This isn't a very long chapter because Credibility is a no-brainer. Why not be true to yourself?

But let me have a little fun and illustrate by using another one of our clients, Dunkin' Donuts,® as an example. Through a lot of interaction and a great deal of time talking to consumers about Dunkin' Donuts® over the past three years, Ken and I have come to think about the Dunkin' Donuts® brand as an "everyday Joe." In fact, it is about the average American, the honest, hard-working guys or girls who get out there everyday and make a living, whether it's in the office, at a barber shop or clothing store, driving an 18-wheeler, or driving their kids to soccer. Dunkin' Donuts® is consistent, reliable, and for millions of

---

Dunkin Donuts ® is a registered trademark of Dunkin Brands, Inc.

people, high quality coffee that's a non-negotiable part of their everyday routine. Dunkin' Donuts® is no nonsense, straightforward, and approachable. It's in and out so that everyday Joes can get on their way and into their day with a good cup of coffee at a good price. Dunkin' Donuts'® recent ad campaign, "*America Runs on Dunkin'*," depicts and personifies that grounding in the everyday energy generated by everyday people just getting out there and getting things done.

If we were to reverse-engineer the Dunkin' Donuts® brand truth reality, it would be something like this:

- *It is:* a simply consistent, quickly delivered, high quality cup of coffee at a reasonable price.

- *It is not:* a pretentious, overly expensive latte that is enjoyed over a long period of time.

- *It stands for:* the everyday hard-working man or woman that makes this country what it is.

- *It stands against:* phoniness, fluff, and being idle and self-indulgent.

- *It's an expert in:* coffee and donuts.

- *It knows nothing about:* skinny soy lattes.

Now, can you guess which brand is the absolute antithesis to Dunkin'? Yep. It's that West Coast–inspired, special sipping, doing nothing, vente double mocha, no-whip, soy skinny latte for $6.00 coffee brand. Now imagine that Dunkin' Donuts® decided it wanted some of that business, and that to do so, it needed to assert a more upscale and self-important imagery. What if it presented itself to consumers (heaven forbid) with the same imagery as that "other" brand? I guarantee you that the consumer response—both Dunkin' customers and competitive customers—would be a resounding, "I don't think so." Or maybe for Dunkin' customers, something more fitting like, "What are you, nuts?" Dunkin' is not like that. It doesn't make sense that they'd assume that position. It's not how consumers think about the brand. It doesn't jive with their experience with the brand. It's simply not credible. And that means the consumer would tune it out. There's already another coffee brand doing that. What's the point? At the risk of sounding repetitive, brands are what they are. Communication that taps into a brand's basic reality is more successful at establishing important relationships because the message is more credible.

There's always an exception . . .

All that said, however, I do have an exception to the Credibility rule. It's in a brand called "Target"—or Tar-*jay,* as it is also lovingly known. It's now an icon. When you see that red bull's-eye, you may remember all the times you've seen it in vast repetition in print, television, billboards, sports arenas, even plastered on floors and walls, and you automatically think "Target." However, do you remember when Target first began to advertise in that hip, funky way? I do. I think it was in the early 1990s and I remember seeing these really cool commercials and print ads filled with ultimately hip looking people doing fabulously hip things and featuring those regular everyday items—like Era Laundry Detergent or Dentyne Chewing Gum—in the coolest, most creative ways. Did I mention *cool* and *hip*? I stress this because in my mind at the time, Target was decidedly *not* cool or hip. To me, it was one of those big-box discounters that sold clothing and yes, laundry detergent of all things, across the aisle from each other! But some brilliant marketing team, which I like to think was fueled or confirmed by some brilliant consumer discovery work, saw an opportunity in the marketplace to position the brand as the cooler, better merchandised alternative to Wal-Mart and Kmart. So why not project a little image superiority here?

However, I remember watching the commercial and thinking to myself, "Yeah, right." Who did they think they were? It's *Target!* They can't credibly project that image. And yet, they kept on doing it. Everywhere I looked I saw those cool, hip Target ads! And I found, after many years, that—darn it! — I did believe that Target was a cool (or at least cool*er*) place to shop for household stuff. What Target successfully did was create Credibility in the area of coolness, even though in my mind it had no Credibility in that territory. It simply assumed the position. And through many years, a variety of media vehicles, a ton of advertising dollars, and most critically, delivering coolness via the in-store experience, it has firmly entrenched itself as the cooler place to shop for everything from soap to stationary to salad spinners. I'd rather go there than to Wal-Mart or Kmart, that's for sure. And the beauty is, there's no stigma in shopping there. In fact, it's so cool, that you actually *want* people to know you shop there! It has evolved its state of "hip" so well that now Target ads don't even feature the products it sells—they're much more about high fashion imagery. Even the media placement defines the ultimate in "edge." I recently saw those red bull's-eyes painted on the stairs at Chicago's Union Station.

Target's positioning is analogous to when you keep saying something over and over out loud that's totally believable to you but may not necessarily be to someone else. Eventually it is likely to sink in because you have faith in it and you speak with conviction about it. So it becomes credible. That's exactly what Target did. It had faith in its presentation, executed it well, and maintained a conviction and consistency of message. Credibility was built.

Looking back on the chronology of events, there are a few key post-scripts to this story. First, when Target decided to create its own cool and hip reality, the position of cool and hip mass merchandiser was unoccupied. At the time, that category space was available to own. Second, the brand was willing to alter its merchandise and in-store experience, featuring fairly well-known American designer names (e.g., Isaac Mizrahi) to deliver on that brand image. And third, Target management was brave enough to reach deep into its pocket of marketing dollars long enough to see it through. At the end of the day, Target sells the same things, more or less, as Wal-Mart. But in the world of mass merchandisers, I think you'll agree that Target is cool and Wal-Mart is decidedly not. *Cool* is now totally credible for Target.

You might be thinking, she just built a case for the Credibility C as being riddled with holes. Well, not exactly. I just built a case for the exception. There's always one. Yes, you can sail against the wind. It just takes longer to get where you're going and the trip becomes more arduous and unpredictable, and likely more expensive. Why risk it?

I maintain that Credibility is a critical C. The audience

may completely understand a communicator's message and even connect with it on an emotional level, then promptly turn around and tell us that coming from this particular source—brand, candidate, whatever—they aren't buying it. The message has not been faithful to this particular brand's truth. So the consumer quite understandably reacts with something like, "Excuse me, but your brand cannot present itself to me in that way because it just doesn't compute." And if that's the case, chances are good the communication will perform in one of two ways on the last "C," Contagiousness, neither of them good. It will not be the least bit contagious because people don't pass along information they believe comes from a dubious source. Or worse yet, it will totally backfire on the brand and generate negative word of mouth instead of the positive variety. Which brings me to the final C.

CHAPTER 6

The Fourth C: Contagiousness

This is just sick.

—Anonymous skateboarder
(and my 11-year-old son)

Of course, we saved what some might consider the best, albeit the most elusive and subjective C for last. In the most rudimentary definition of the word "contagious," it means "infectious," something that gets spread from one being or entity to another. Something (or someone) that if you get too close to, you might catch it.

We usually think of "contagious" as being bad, but in communications, Contagiousness is a good thing. You want your audience to "catch it." In fact, you want them to catch it, run with it, and spread it around, which is most unlikely to happen without the first three Cs. The audience needs to understand the message, relate to it because it speaks to them in a way that matters, and believe it in order for it to be memorable and have the kind of emotional impact that leads to Contagiousness.

Human beings are social animals. That's pretty well documented. When something interests us we can't wait to share it with others. When it doesn't, we could care less. And heaven forbid, if it fails the Credibility test badly enough, we may want to share it in the worst possible way—by actively debunking it!

This last C is both the most mysterious and the most fascinating to us, because much as virologists still struggle to understand how viruses hijack our DNA to serve their own nefarious purposes, communications professionals struggle to understand what makes certain messages, or the way they're delivered, so darn "catchy."

What made the Budweiser *Whassup!* campaign such an overnight sensation? Why did *Just Do It* do it so well for Nike? (So much so that Coke shifted $150 million in advertising to its creators in hopes that some of that same magic might rub off.) You don't need to be a political scientist to appreciate what "It's the economy, stupid" brought to Bill Clinton's first campaign. Or what "Show me the money!" did for *Jerry Maguire*. Or, as discussed in greater detail in chapter 11, what the movies *Brokeback Mountain* and *Crash* did for their respective movie studio's bottom lines.

Contagiousness is the "special sauce" of effective communications—imbuing the message, idea, or image with a unique and memorable "flavor." This chapter will delve into how and why that's the case. It will also show how difficult it can be to achieve, which is why many communications efforts manage to accomplish decent results without it. However, in a qualitative environment when the room starts buzzing, when the respondents start talking among themselves about what they've just seen, when the energy level is palpable, you know the communication is on its way to becoming an unqualified success. I've found that Contagiousness, in the positive sense, is often intimately linked to Connection. When a message truly resonates with its audience in a profound, "sink into the bones" way, there tends to be a residual Contagiousness effect. They simply can't help thinking about it or mentioning it in conversation. Remember my Suave example, "That's me, that's me, that's me!" For that moment, right there in the room, that woman got excited about the message. She spoke out, her voice rose, she pointed to each ad; she was infected. The brand had found an idea that not only resonated with its target—Moms want pretty hair too!—but executed it in a way that left the recipient feeling empowered and excited by the message. The Suave brand now has the opportunity to sink in with this target—to "infect" the way she thinks about the brand. That's Contagiousness.

Let's go back to that Dove® "Real Women/Campaign for Real Beauty." Talk about contagious. That campaign has infiltrated TV shows, talk shows, the monologues of late night talk show hosts, and magazine editorials. It just doesn't stop. Maybe you've seen or at least heard of the 90-second Dove® video, *Evolution,* developed and produced by Ogilvy & Mather in Toronto and shown on YouTube. It is a visually fascinating account of how one otherwise average looking woman, through the miracles of make-up, professional hair-styling, and some masterful retouching, morphs into a beautiful supermodel. The October 30, 2006 edition of *Advertising Age* calls it "a web spot that has gone megaviral." Again, you get a message that connects on that deeper level and you get a Contagiousness factor. This is the stuff that seeps into consumers' psyches. It becomes part of their culture. That's Contagiousness on steroids! And in this case, Contagiousness in the consumer world also panned out in the world of marketing evaluation. For 2005, the Dove® "Campaign for Real Beauty" campaign won the Grand Effie, the top advertising award conferred by the American Marketing Association for great ideas that achieve real results. It's the marketing industry's version of the Academy Awards. Now the Dove® campaign is certifiably contagious.

In keeping with the Dove® brand (yes, I have been fortunate enough to have spent many years working on several parts of this great brand), let me give you another example of a contagious communication idea. A couple of years ago, when introducing its line of hair-styling products into a vast ocean of styling products, Dove® needed to make a mark. Its advertising agency, Ogilvy & Mather/Chicago, came up with a brilliant communication idea. Why not look at famous "hairstyle-challenged" cartoon characters and use them to show the abilities and benefits of the Dove® styling aids? I bet you can already imagine some great examples of cartoon characters that would fit the description. One great and obvious example is Marge Simpson. Marge, who gives a unique and limitless definition to the phrase "high hair," and paints a younger picture of that "blue-haired lady" image, is a quintessential icon of the hair-challenged. Brilliant. And that's exactly what consumers thought. Showing Marge Simpson's hair in magazines, on bus shelters, sides of buses, and shopping mall kiosks transformed from a starch-stiff blue totem pole to long, free-flowing, bouncy and beautifully touchable blue locks. Not only, as you might imagine, was it a highly arresting visual, but it was a very persuasive and believable message. If those products could do that for Marge Simpson's hair, imagine what they can do for me? The overall campaign was perceived by consumers to be a fresh, innovative approach to talking about hair care products. A direct quote from one consumer was, "It sticks in your mind . . . I'd probably talk about it to my friends." Truly contagious.

Being contagious is what I like to do

Let's move on to another of our favorite brands, Dunkin' Donuts.® After a few years of dancing around a great advertising idea, this venerated and much loved brand has now landed on a truly infectious idea: "*America Runs on Dunkin*'." You may have seen one of its quirky and highly memorable television ads, and found yourself humming one of those quirky and highly memorable tunes, like, "Doing things is what I like to do—YES!"

And maybe you've also seen the Dunkin' Donuts® *KA-RAH-TAAAY!* commercial, which is in and of itself infectious. The ad features a typical suburban "soccer mom" driving a minivan filled with five activity-oriented kids. The ad begins with a quick, catchy, percussive beat. We see a hand as it puts a plastic cup of a Dunkin' Donuts® strawberry Smoothie back in the cup holder. Now imagine your toe tapping as a combination of hushed voices start to run through the litany of her kids' activities, all the while keeping quick time with the beat. "Swimming, soccer, ballet, oboe," and as each activity is ticked off the camera cuts to the respective kid dressed for his or her activity. Then we get to "—and last but not least" at which time the camera quickly cuts to the mom who stares straight at the camera and lip syncs as the voiceover screams, "KA-RAH-TAAAY!" And then, in case we didn't laugh enough the first time, it starts again, cutting to the same kid visuals as the voiceover repeats, "swimming, soccer, ballet, oboe—and just one more time," and back to the mom again for "KA-RAH-TAAAY!" The first time I saw it, not only did I find it hysterical, but I found myself saying "KA-RAH-TAAAY!" from time to time for the next few days.

And just so you can rest assured that Contagiousness isn't only measured by winning Grand Effie awards and humming a tune to yourself in the middle of your day, here's an example of a contagious package element. A new package graphic for the beloved children's brand, Popsicle, featured a turtle as an icon to showcase its long lasting benefit. In getting feedback from moms about the packaging, the energy and interest in the room shot way up when it came to the turtle. It seemed he was not only a fun way to personify "long lasting," but he was also perceived to be kid-friendly and absolutely adorable! The moms wanted to name him, to dress him, to create a personality for him by adding some "word bubbles" over his head! Right there in the room, he was becoming known as "that Popsicle turtle." Now that's contagious—a new way to think about Popsicle established in about 30 minutes.

The criterion for Contagiousness doesn't mean that you need to stand on chairs and scream about what a great message you just heard or experienced. Or that you would

instantly call your best friend on the phone and say, "Hey—
I just saw this great new package that I just HAVE to tell
you about!" Get serious. To have a good idea of whether
or not a piece of communiqué is truly contagious, you need
to ask yourself these questions:

- Is there a sense of *energy* around the message and
  the way it is executed?

- Does it offer a new way to view the brand or category?

- Is it competitively differentiating?

- Is there something innately *memorable* about it?

- Does it evoke a vivid *emotional* response? (that may
  not always be positive)

- Might it have talk potential? (again, it may not be
  positive talk)

- Does it motivate the target to *do something?*

- Does it elicit some kind of highly charged demon-
  strable and visible reaction?

If your communication can say "yes" to even a few of
these questions, then it just might be on the verge of
Contagiousness, which—assuming it is also clearly comprehended, connects with its target, and is nod-your-head-
credible—means it just might be on the path to effective
communication. While this may all sound like an entirely
logical, rational process, it is and it isn't. Now let's take a
look at the all-important role of the "right side" of the brain.

CHAPTER 7

I've Got This Feeling . . .

The truth is rarely pure and never simple.

—Oscar Wilde

Wouldn't it be nice if people always behaved in an entirely logical fashion? If all our actions and beliefs never deviated from a rational path? That would sure make Aristotle's day. Not to mention Descartes's and the legions of 20th-century economists' who tried mightily to convince us that there was such a thing as *"Homo economicus"*—that individuals always found and followed the decision tree that logically leads to their best interest.

Alas, that just doesn't seem to be the case. Behavioral economists Robert J. Aumann and Thomas C. Schelling, who won the 2005 Nobel Prize "for having enhanced our understanding of conflict and cooperation through game theory analysis," demonstrated that people are often decidedly illogical and frankly, downright perplexing in some of the decisions they make about the value of money. One example is the study that showed a majority of people would prefer to make $100,000 a year in a community where the average salary was $50,000 a year instead of $200,000 in a community where the average salary was $300,000. Now, how much sense does that make? Speaking rationally, people can buy twice as much stuff in the latter case, yet they prefer the former. Possibly because there's a whole lot more to it than purely rational analysis. All of this raises some interesting questions about the 4Cs approach. People aren't entirely rational. In fact, I'd say that it is part of the human condition to often act in irrational ways. Any research methodology is remiss if it doesn't take this into account.

Up until now it has probably seemed like the 4Cs process is incredibly rational. It is step-by-step, very methodical, and left-brained almost to a fault. But I won't apologize for that. Most marketers, myself included, are classically trained business school–types, some of whom may have a bias toward the analytical and are thus quite comfortable with a process that resembles the Boston Consulting Group matrix mentioned in the preface. On the other hand, I'm not oblivious to what's been going on in the study of how the brain works and the biochemical role emotion plays in the way people react to communications. All of this brings me to two almond-shaped organs deep inside the brain, one in each hemisphere, known as the amygdalae. I've learned just enough about them to be dangerous.

Leap before you look

With the development of new tools like "functional magnetic resonance imaging" (MRI) devices, the people who study how our brains work are getting a better and better picture (pun intended) of how our gray matter actually deals with stimuli—or what we in the communications world call "information," "advertising," "packaging," or the like. And in the process, they've validated what poets and artists have known intuitively for millennia. Every bit of stimuli we take in triggers an emotional and potentially irrational reaction long before it's transformed into a logical "reason." By now, we know this all too well. What you may not know is that this is the effect of the amygdala. There's simply no escaping this mechanism. Every piece of stimuli, from the snaky-looking stick we talked about in chapter 2, to your new ad campaign is going to elicit a profoundly emotional response several nanoseconds before it gets its rational overlay. I sometimes think it's like a thunderstorm. We hear the thunder because it's so loud, but it actually comes several seconds later than the lightning and is, in fact, caused by the lightning; it is not an independent event.

"Blink" is right

So if we take it as a scientific given that anything we do or say to our audience is going to produce an irrational, visceral, potentially hostile, and frequently unconscious response, we need to know what that is, don't we? And short of conducting all our Truth Discovery Sessions inside a gigantic MRI machine, how the heck are we supposed to do that?

Well it's simple, and my colleagues in consumer insight discovery will recognize this all too well. We ask people to whom we've just shown some communication stimulus for their "gut reaction," that is, the first thing they *feel* about a piece of communication. We instruct them not to think, just feel. To borrow a page from Malcolm Gladwell's book, we're looking for their "blink" reaction. "Snap!" Just like that. You can only do this for a few seconds immediately after exposure and then the moment is gone. And thereafter throughout the discussion, there will never be another chance to have a "gut" reaction.

Truth is stranger (and harder to get at) than fiction

You see, the point of this entire exercise is to capture peoples' initial, and one might say, *primal* reaction to a piece of communication—a TV spot, print ad, packaging sample, tag line, logo design, whatever—before it's clouded or sullied by a bunch of "groupthink," "over think," or just plain peer pressure.

I think of it as a form of crowd control for these sessions, but it's also a valuable type of truth serum. In the post discussion analysis of what these consumers write down, I sometimes discover that the way some respondents articulated their "gut" reaction to the group seems at great odds with what they wrote down as an initial "gut" reaction. It's not that people are inherently dishonest. It's just that we often have a tough time not being swayed by others and frequently lose sight of our own personal truth. In fact, it's not uncommon, after hearing someone else say something that sounds particularly astute or perceptive, for people to revise their "gut" reaction, which you can't truly do. Of course, it's quite understandable, but it is no measure of a true "gut" reaction.

So for the 4Cs of Truth in Communications to work, we have to get to the heart of the matter, the gut or emotional underpinning of what people are saying in response to a particular stimulus. If something was genuinely comprehended, we need to know the *what* and *why*. If something truly connected, we need to understand what deep down emotional truth is causing the inherent Connection. If there's a lot of Contagiousness to an idea, we have to be sure it was the idea that did it, not the discussion that took place afterwards. All of which reminds me of a movie every seeker of the truth, student of human nature, or marketer should see at least once a year.

Twelve Angry Men

The parallel between what I'm trying to do and what this classic movie is about strikes me as ironic.

In the film, a first-time directorial *tour de force* by Sidney Pollack, a panoply of the greatest stars, future stars, and character actors of the late 1950s is empanelled as a jury chosen to decide the guilt or innocence of a poor Hispanic kid accused of murdering his father. After a cursory discussion of the evidence, the first vote is taken, with the jury coming in at something like ten to two in favor of conviction.

However, one character, played by Henry Fonda, isn't quite so sure. As the story unfolds, the other jurors can't help but reveal the emotional, "gut" underpinnings that totally swayed their initial verdicts. Slowly but surely, they come to question their first reactions and ultimately change their minds. It's a gripping drama. But more importantly to me, and the subject of this book, it's incredibly instructive, because that's what my clients and *every* client should be looking for: an honest verdict.

Is this a piece of communication you should invest one million, ten million, a hundred million dollars in, or isn't it? If it is, why? How could it be made an even better investment? Where are its weaknesses (surely it has a few), and what can you do about them? If it isn't worth investing in, why not? And what should you do about it? That's the entire *raison d'etre* to this process.

On the surface, it might appear that the 4Cs approach is rooted in "left brain" soil. But surface appearances can be deceiving. Yes, it is a logical approach, but in order to truly evaluate stand-out effective communication using The 4Cs of Truth in Communications, both sides of brain must be fully engaged and aware.

By the same token, it might also be tempting to classify the 4Cs as something that is strictly confined to the evaluation of traditional advertising communication. In fact, as the next chapter illustrates, it may surprise you how many forms of communication to which this evaluative approach can be applied.

CHAPTER 8

The 4Cs: They're Not Just For Advertising Anymore

Truth is always exciting. Speak it then.
Life is boring without it

—Pearl S. Buck

It would be safe to assume at this point that the 4Cs work well at evaluating the effectiveness of traditional media communications. But what marketer is limiting him or herself to that? If anything, non-traditional media is today getting a great deal of marketers' attention and is being charged with accounting for a great deal of brand awareness, brand equity and of course, brand sales.

The 4Cs meet I, P & L

Not too long ago, we were asked to help our client, Dollar Rent A Car, evaluate its primary marketing effort—its website. The objectives were to better understand the answers to questions such as: what are their users' specific needs when renting online? How can the website be made easier to use and understand so it is more appealing to the user? The company wanted to understand how the site's design stacked up against the competitive landscape and most importantly, how to identify areas of opportunity for improved communications, ease of use, and visual design.

We were given three home page options (Figure 8.1) to explore with consumers. In each case, our mission was, as always, to determine if the main page's message was being *communicated* clearly; if the message resonated or *connected* with the audience and if so, what was driving this connection and motivating usage. Was the design *credible* for Dollar and to what degree was the site *contagious*—meaning in this case, memorable, competitively differentiated, and a site that you'd likely recommend to someone else and continue to use the next time you were in the market for a rental car.

In this instance, there was no clear winner. However, Option 2 came closest to communicating with the consumer on several levels. There was some considerable

FIGURE 8.1

Option 1   Option 2

work however, that needed to be addressed within each C. Comprehension was heavily reliant on how well the information was presented in visual "blocks." This presentation made the consumers' understanding of the message clearer and easier. There was an opportunity to increase the Connection with and engagement in the site by providing bolder, more vivid graphics throughout. In the area of Credibility, Dollar was missing the opportunity to drive home (pun intended) its brand's unassailable truth. It is primarily known as an economical car rental brand and yet all its communication about great deals and good value seemed to be buried within a lot of other things happening on the page. And there was a lot of room for improvement in Contagiousness if the site could offer those who perused it "a little something extra," for their time on the webpage, like hotel recommendations, travel directions, or weather forecasts for a particular city. The site could make visitors think of Dollar Rent A Car in a new and different way, to increase their energy around the brand.

Option 3

So, do the 4Cs have street cred?

Dollar Rent A Car is one example of how the 4Cs have been used to help evaluate the world of "clicks," but what about the world of "bricks," like on-site communications? Our client, Togo's® Sandwich Shop, gave us the opportunity to test the 4Cs at the grassroots level.

Togo's® was embarking on a significant change of the brand's overall market position, a direct result of positioning work we did which helped to provide a clear and credible new direction. This included re-evaluating many marketing components, including its brand logo and menu board designs to determine which fit best with the new positioning direction. Togo's® presented us with three logo designs as well as two menu boards to discuss with consumers. But before you glance over the logo stimuli on the next page, keep this in mind. The Togo's® brand has an extremely limited advertising budget, so its logo is one of its primary marketing elements. As such, it is responsible for not only drawing the consumer into the store but establishing a brand essence, creating a consumer relationship and inviting them to return there instead of going to Subway. Now that's a lot to ask for a graphic design, so you can imagine that discovering the right logo was critical to the brand's successful re-launch.

And if you'll look at Figure 8.2, which provides a side-by-side 4Cs analysis of each logo, you'll see what we found. No clear winner across targets, but clear direction for re-design. The final logo, you'll see (Figure 8.3), draws a great deal from the learning from the "surfboard" logo, incorporating its Contagiousness strengths of being com-

---

Togo's® Sandwich Shop is a registered trademark of Dunkin Brands, Inc.

petitively differentiating, active, contemporary and ener-
getic, while strengthening its communication of "sandwich"
and removing the confusing water imagery. Further, it
draws learning from the "bread head" logo's lower case,
more contemporary, and generally cooler looking typeface.

FIGURE 8.2

The 4Cs of Truth in Communications Evaluation for Togo's® Logos

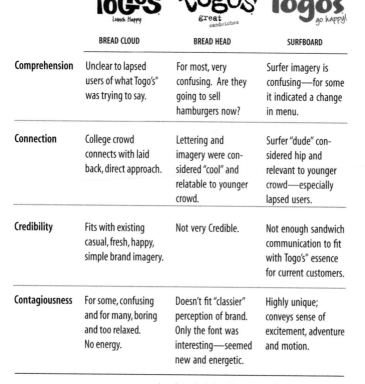

	BREAD CLOUD	BREAD HEAD	SURFBOARD
Comprehension	Unclear to lapsed users of what Togo's® was trying to say.	For most, very confusing. Are they going to sell hamburgers now?	Surfer imagery is confusing—for some it indicated a change in menu.
Connection	College crowd connects with laid back, direct approach.	Lettering and imagery were considered "cool" and relatable to younger crowd.	Surfer "dude" considered hip and relevant to younger crowd—especially lapsed users.
Credibility	Fits with existing casual, fresh, happy, simple brand imagery.	Not very Credible.	Not enough sandwich communication to fit with Togo's® essence for current customers.
Contagiousness	For some, confusing and for many, boring and too relaxed. No energy.	Doesn't fit "classier" perception of brand. Only the font was interesting—seemed new and energetic.	Highly unique; conveys sense of excitement, adventure and motion.

Logo designs by Graham & Wayman, www.GrahamandWayman.com

FIGURE 8.3   Final Logo

Firing on all Cs

On the other hand, the 4Cs analysis often leads to an absolute answer, as it did for the two examples that follow.

The Breyers® Ice Cream brand needed to differentiate the packaging of its new "extra creamy" formulation from its basic brand packaging. In qualitative exposure of its new packaging (Figures 8.4 & 8.5), we ran the consumer feedback through the 4Cs framework and what we learned proved to be quite enlightening and provided great direction for optimization on each C:

- *Comprehension:* There was an opportunity for the package to communicate "extra creamy" more overtly so consumers get it right away. And the milk pitcher was confusing and didn't add anything to help communicate "extra creamy."

- *Connection:* The idea of "extra creamy" resonates strongly with ice cream lovers. It implies more enjoyment, and motivates consumers to want to try it.

- *Credibility:* Among loyal Breyers® users, there was a bit of an issue with the absence of the "all natural" claim.

- *Contagiousness:* The new package color helped to differentiate from the base brand and implied a "creamy" taste.

Ultimately, the 4Cs evaluation helped lead to a package design that was not only different from the base brand's package, thus achieving the objective, but perhaps more importantly, the end package result (Figure 8.6) acknowledged and incorporated much of the learning of the 4Cs for communication.

FIGURE 8.4 Original Extra Creamy Packaging

FIGURE 8.5 4C-Tested Revised Extra Creamy Packaging

FIGURE 8.6 The Final Package Incorporates 4Cs learning:

- Emphasizes and explains "extra creamy"
- Milk pitcher signals a more "homemade" product
- Package color helps differentiate from parent "black box"

STOUFFER'S,® on the other hand, provides an example of an even earlier point on the brand marketing food chain, the optimal positioning. STOUFFER'S® was introducing a new "panini-style" frozen sandwich line and needed help to determine which positioning (from three options) to move forward with prior to quantitative concept testing. We exposed consumers to three different product concept ideas. The following demonstrates how the feedback to the "restaurant/bistro style" concept (Figure 8.8) was evaluated using the 4Cs framework. And you'll see, by glancing at Figure 8.8, how it was ultimately executed in the marketplace.

- *Comprehension:* Communicates well the idea of "restaurant-style sandwiches at home."

- *Connection:* Single, upscale adults connect with this concept best, since it provides for them a valuable benefit of meal replacement.

- *Credibility:* The STOUFFER'S,® brand is highly credible in the areas of take-out chain-restaurant meals, and high-quality frozen products. The idea of a "restaurant-style" frozen sandwich from this brand made total sense.

- *Contagiousness:* This product was interesting because it was a new product concept in a newly created category of frozen foods. The "bistro" comparison imbues the STOUFFER'S® brand with a much-needed younger, hipper, and even higher quality imagery.

STOUFFER'S® and CORNER BISTRO® are registered trademarks of Société des Produits, Nestlé S.A., Vevey, Switzerland

FIGURE 8.7

Concept-Tested Positioning

For adults looking to satisfy more sophisticated (complex) taste expectations from the meals they enjoy at home, STOUFFER'S® new Panini-style sandwiches are the first frozen sandwiches with the fresh-grilled taste and textures of their favorite restaurant sandwich. Because only STOUFFER'S® Panini-style sandwiches provide select, fresh-quality meats, aged cheeses and sautéed herbs and vegetables prepared on a variety of distinctive breads with a bakery-fresh taste. These sandwiches actually grill up in the microwave for a satisfying taste and texture that's crispy on the outside and tender on the inside.

FIGURE 8.8   The Final Package In-market

CHAPTER 9

E-Me. Feel Me. Touch Me.

Man is least himself when he talks in his own person. Give him a mask, and he will tell you the truth.

—Oscar Wilde

Any 21st-century discussion of communication would be remiss if it didn't address what has probably become the single most pervasive form of communication going. Whether you e-mail, text message, instant message, blog, or hawk your "wares" on MySpace or eBay, you are a member of the electronic sub-culture. Anyone who spends time on the internet cannot help but get inundated with SPAM messages and pop-up ads. Electronic messaging continues to surge. Between emails, text messages, LED boards, pop-up ads and the like, we are exposed to literally hundreds of electronic messages every day.

But electronic messaging is not limited to having access to a computer or the internet. All you have to do is simply look out your office windows or drive a block or two from your home into town and you'll see those LED Electronic Message Reader Boards that flash the latest bank rates, the breaking news, the current weather and time, and the latest movement in the Dow Jones Industrial Average. Drive by many high schools and colleges and you're likely to see an electronic message board right under the name of the school communicating registration deadlines, holiday schedules, and the names of the students who won a recent athletic competition or scored especially high on their SATs. And all this electronic messaging isn't something entirely new. If you think about the most quintessential electronic message reader board—the one located in Times Square in New York City—you'll have to think back 75 years to track its debut! Electronic messaging is not only pervasive, it is enduring. And it is a perfect subject for a 4Cs analysis.

Email mania

I'm not the first to write about the delicate nature of email communication, and I likely won't be the last. While it is tempting to be lured into thinking an email message is just like having a conversation, it isn't. Conversations are spoken—they have the benefit of tone of voice, inflection, and if someone misunderstands, the opportunity for instant clarification. This is always a critical distinction from the written word, where nuances in voice inflection that convey a tongue-in-cheek "I'm just kidding," or a dead-serious "I really mean this," obviously don't exist. Email messages are more likely to be taken very literally—they can be saved and scrutinized over and over. They can be passed from the intended recipient to the unintended. In fact, if not executed correctly, email messaging can backfire on its intent, threaten relationships, and even endanger careers.

Enter The 4Cs of Truth in Communication. Let's take Comprehension. This is always an obvious one, but it's important that the reader simply understands the message contained in the email. And this has everything to do with language, vocabulary, punctuation (which we don't have to worry about using the spoken word), and tone. It is highly important that the proper tone be *understood* when reading an email message. One great way of ensuring instant comprehension is the subject line. Think about it. Other than the sender's name, it's the only piece of information readers see before they open the email. Therein lies the opportunity to either invite him into your message and open it, or "save it" for later. And you know what that means? The likelihood that it will get read in the future is about 50 percent.

A friend and colleague of mine with whom I hadn't communicated recently sent me an email with the subject message "let's get together for breakfast!" So I immediately understood, even before opening the email, what the purpose of her message was. And the exclamation point communicated to me that she was enthusiastic about the prospect of getting together. That's a great start. On the other hand, when I get an email that says "no subject"—even if I know the sender, I'm not as eager to open it and may skip over it. So, it is important that your subject line contain a message that is clearly comprehensible, interesting, relevant, and motivating—which touches on Comprehension, Connection, and Contagiousness.

Let's look more deeply into *Connection*. Remember the

key question we ask about Connection? *Is the message speaking to them on a personal level? Does it really matter to them?* If the message is not relevant, doesn't address a topic or area of concern or interest on a rational or emotional level, then it's not making a Connection. Think about the number of times you press the "delete" button just by seeing some words in a subject line that are frivolous, not interesting, or otherwise irrelevant to you. For instance, whenever I got an email from the publishers of this book that said "your book," I was inherently interested. It made an immediate and critical Connection for me—both rationally and emotionally. Obviously, this is something that *matters* to me. Email messages need to connect on a personal level too.

What about *Credibility?* This is critical. Think back to the "who," "what," and "how" assessments we use to determine Credibility.

- **Who?** Does the message make sense coming from this brand—or in this case, the sender? Or on an even broader, more relative "cut," *is the sender himself credible?* We know that if we don't recognize the sender or are not making a Connection with the subject line, it's not even worth opening the email.

- **What?** Is it something the audience [reader] expects from this brand [sender]? If the message, or more importantly, the *tone* doesn't sync with expectations, the message is likely to lose Credibility.

- **How?** Is the message executed in a way that fits with the brand's [sender's] equity with its audience [reader]?

It's obviously critical that both the sender and the email message are credible to deliver an effective email message.

Now what about *Contagiousness?* Here again, another tricky area. But let's think about it. This is the area where tone, which in my mind is one of the most important components of email communication, steps in and takes charge. If the tone of your email message is exciting, motivating, or differentiating, it's likely to deliver your message effectively. Remember my example of my friend's invitation to breakfast? The tone was definitely motivating to me. Again, recalling some of the questions we use to assess the Contagiousness factor, think about the potential effectiveness of your next email message in terms of:

- *Energy.* Is there a sense of energy around the message? Is there something in the headline or opening sentence that makes the reader want to continue reading?

- *Newsworthy.* Does it offer a new way to view the brand [sender]? This will likely mean the message and/or the sender is more memorable.

- *Unique.* Is it competitively differentiating? Does it stand out from the hundreds of other emails in the readers' in-box that week? Obviously, there's an opportunity to do this in the subject line as well.

- *Emotionally-charged.* Does it evoke a vivid emotional response? Here's an example how if your tone is off, the emotional response may be completely negative.

- *Motivation.* Does it motivate the target to *do something?* Will the target hit "reply," or "delete"?

In fact, I would maintain that when it comes to effective electronic communication, tone is one of the most critical and most difficult to accurately execute. Come to think of it, misconstrued tonality of an email—or any electronic—message can adversely affect all the Cs.

Instant. Now. Turbo!

Steven Wright, a comedian popular in the late 1980's, had this one joke I thought was hilarious and remains one of the few jokes I can consistently remember. He delivered it as part of a litany of one-liners in his droll, nasally, monotone, stand-up routine. "One morning I put instant coffee in a microwave oven. I almost went back in time."

One of the clear characteristics of many forms of electronic messaging is the instantaneous communication it allows. Text messages or instant messages, for instance, are two forms of communication with a language and a set of communication criteria all their own. Text messaging communicates a message very quickly, using the least number of keyboard characters as possible, knowing that many people may be reading the message at the same time. The very nature of instant messaging (IMing) and text messaging sets up a stark communication challenge. It means you've got to communicate *very* clearly. You've got to be *instantly* understood, say something *instantly* meaningful, be *instantly* recognizable and "worth it" to the reader, and your message needs to be *instantly* motivating and exciting. All that makes an email look easy!

Come to think of it, maybe there's a lesson for "regular" communication we can all take from instant messaging.

Keep the message short, relevant, easily understandable, and to the point. "Can't wait 2G2 Movies w/U 2NITE!" communicates everything—the event, the date, the interest, excitement, and anticipation. Some instant/text messages aren't so easy. "G2G POS" is not as instantly telegraphic, but to the recipient, it's all he needs to know to log off. (In case you were wondering, it means, "Got to go. Parent over shoulder.")

I found IT!

Ah yes, the world of eBay—a veritable marketplace of trade, barter, bidding, and commerce that sells a mind-boggling mix of new and used items ranging from old, empty beer cans to a round of golf with Tiger Woods ($425,000!) to fully-stocked yachts, and draws a worldwide shopping audience of millions each day. An entire industry has emerged from the internet through buying, selling, even packing and shipping on eBay. So how might The 4Cs of Truth in Communication help make this busy marketplace buzz even better? Or, if you're an eBay junkie (and you know who you are), how can you be sure that what you want to sell sells, or if you're buying, you get what you paid for?

Let's say you want to sell a sweater. Are you clearly communicating the features and benefits of the sweater in a clear and concise way (Comprehension)? Are you doing so using language that really matters to the buyer, e.g. telling the buyer how warm, high-quality, and attractive the sweater is (Connection)? Are you doing it in a believable way with supporting information so that the buyer will believe that your sweater is what you say it is? And how is your feedback rating from previous customers (Credibility)? Does the message convey how special and different your sweater is, such that the buyer will notice and remember your sweater amidst all of the other sweaters on the website? Can you ensure that buying from you will be a pleasant, hassle-free experience so that the buyer will be inclined to leave you a positive rating that may influence other potential buyers (Contagiousness)?

What about if you're a buyer? You need to know exactly what it is you're getting. That's Comprehension. And the seller needs to communicate the information about the product in a way that truly matters to you (Connection). The seller needs to convince you that what he or she is saying about the item for sale is true (Credibility) or you will just scroll down to the next similar item listed in that particular section. Perhaps hitting on the first three points will pique your interest, but what will get you to raise the bid and compete for the item is establishing just how special, rare, and different this item is, and/or why you should want to buy it from this unique seller. This is the elusive Contagiousness C and the one that can often tip the scale.

My husband (an eBay junkie who collects antique beer and liquor advertising—don't ask) says he has seen virtually the same item sell for twice as much as another similar one the week before, based largely on the quality of the description of the item proffered by the seller. If he sees an item for sale that is potentially interesting but does not carry a description that inherently addresses the 4Cs, he asks a lot of questions of the seller (if he's *really* interested), but more often than not he just moves on. The seller has failed to successfully communicate the meaningful information, connect with this potential buyer, generate trust, or pique interest in his product.

Some lingering questions

So, now that you've seen how well the 4Cs perform against a wide range of marketing communication vehicles, I feel obligated to answer some frequently asked questions which often come up in any discussion of this framework.

- Is one C more valuable than the other?
- Is there a hierarchy of C significance?
- What if my communications do well on two or three, but not all 4Cs?

CHAPTER 10

Are All Cs Created Equal?

All truths are easy to understand once they are discovered. The point is to discover them.

—Galileo Galilei

Or put another way: Is there one C that stands head and shoulders above the rest in importance? Wouldn't that be nice, because then if your communication really nailed that C, you wouldn't have to worry so much about the others. Sadly, that simply isn't the case.

Contagiousness, as I said earlier, is certainly the most elusive and potentially, the most valuable. But without all the other Cs—Comprehension, Connection and Credibility —pure Contagiousness can be a real trap, as beer advertisers like Miller Genuine Draft may have experienced.

For years this brand marketed itself using an approach that has proved highly contagious among men, its primary audience, since the beginning of time: scantily clad women with made-to-order physical attributes frolicking in all sorts of provocative situations. You can't get much more conta-gious than that.

But by creating an emotional brand Connection and Credibility that relied more heavily on testosterone than hops and barley, combined with the fact that several other beer advertisers were relying on the same sort of "infec-tion," after several years of this, Miller Genuine Draft began, in my opinion, to lose its Contagiousness factor. In fact, it finally had to say goodbye to the "Girls Gone Wild" approach and resort to a more product-focused story, pre-sumably as a way to arrest the brand's share decline and reclaim its unique brand character.

Another classic example of Contagiousness gone awry could be Alka-Seltzer. At one point, more than 25 years ago, this brand was running some of the funniest, most popular TV commercials on the air. At the time it was said the commercials were more popular than much of the pro-gramming. Surely some of you must remember or have seen *I can't believe I ate the whole thing,* or, *Mama mia, that'sa some speecy, spicy meat-a-ball.*

They were truly innovative spots at the time. Those famous lines became part of the vernacular. But ultimately, the advertising failed to escalate the brand to the number one in market share. Why? I'd venture to say there were three reasons:

1. The product's claim lacked Credibility since other products had supplanted Alka-Seltzer as the best pal-liative to indigestion.

2. The situations were of marginal personal Connection since peoples' eating habits were trending sharply away from over-indulgence.

3. The product form and heretofore unique reason for being—tablets that fizzed as they dissolved in water to be drunk—was now relatively cumbersome and seemed out of date, more associated with the likes of Bromo Seltzer than with the more convenient, discreet, and tastier Rolaids.

So while the commercials were funny and very contagious, Alka-Seltzer sat on the shelves gathering dust and only the older, die-hard fizz fans.

Some incredible mistakes

Okay, so if Contagiousness alone isn't enough, what about *Credibility*? Well, Credibility is more a cost-of-entry concept. If a piece of communication is completely incredible, in this case meaning impossible to believe, not great or terrific, trouble is sure to follow.

This is the problem that has dogged most American car manufacturers for decades. *Pontiac. We build excitement.* Yeah, right. Like Tiger Woods would ever have anything to do with a Buick aside from cashing their checks. And if *At Ford, quality is job 1,* then why were they forced to shed job numbers 2 to 20,000 not long ago?

Incredibility can also have more subtle, but equally dangerous implications. Remember *The softer side of Sears*? This was a great attempt to reposition the Sears brand away from being only about circular saws and washing machines to something "softer" and more JCPenny-like—which included clothing, cosmetics and housewares. Very nice advertising. Kind of cool. Very fashionable. Even a little on the sexy side. The trouble was none of this manifested itself in the way the store was merchandised—from the "uniform" of the employees that worked there, to the stores' locations, or even the brand logo, which still sat atop many old brown buildings in those big block letters. Not at all "soft" looking to me.

The flip side of this is being genuinely credible and even having that sneak up and bite you. Let's look at BP. I'm willing to give the brand the benefit of the doubt and acknowledge that its "Beyond Petroleum" ecologically sensitive position was truly heartfelt, but when BP experienced a spate of environmental disasters, what happened? The media had a field day making mincemeat out of BP, taking it way "beyond petroleum."

I get it already, now will you please go away

Comprehension is another sort of no-brainer, cost-of-entry C. If the audience doesn't understand your intended message, that can't be good. However, Comprehension is only the beginning.

Most of the leading packaged-goods marketers and, in fact, a vast majority of mainstream advertisers are famous for employing all sorts of copy testing methodologies to ensure that the TV spot on which they're about to spend $25 to 50 million is clearly comprehended. Unfortunately, many of the commercials that pass these tests with flying colors are so singularly lacking in interest and excitement (i.e., Connection and Contagiousness) that without that much spent behind them it's doubtful they'd ever work. And many still don't.

One of my alma maters in the advertising business is the agency Ted Bates, which spawned the likes of Rosser

Reeves, legendary agency guy who invented the USP or "unique selling proposition," and was all about the "hit-em-over-the-head" communication technique. In fact, Reeves wrote a great little book entitled, *Reality in Advertising,* which espoused the philosophy, "buy this product and you will get this specific benefit." Ted Bates was well-known in the agency business for the crystalline comprehensibility of its advertising, sometimes to the point that its USP might have shown a little too clearly! You will surely recall some of these brilliant USP-driven taglines: *Wonder Builds Strong Bodies in 12 Ways; The Milk Chocolate Melts in Your Mouth, Not in Your Hand; It's Two Mints in One,* and *How Do You Spell Relief?*

There's some advertising running right now that's straight out of the Ted Bates/Rosser Reeves school. You might have seen it: *HeadOn—apply directly to the forehead. HeadOn—apply directly to the forehead. HeadOn—apply directly to the forehead.* Hard to misunderstand that one, but maybe after awhile, even harder to stand it. In fact, interestingly, HeadOn has recently modified this approach so that now after a couple of stanzas of that annoying litany, a person walks on camera and basically says, "*HeadOn, your commercials are so annoying, but your product is wonderful.*" I don't think this was part of the original communication strategy, nor is it an example of Comprehension alone building a power brand franchise.

Operator, I think I've been disconnected

Finally, there's the matter of *Connection,* which as I've said repeatedly throughout this book, walks hand in hand with Contagiousness through the valley of value and importance.

Yet, once again, Connection alone is not enough and can even be dangerous if handled improperly.

As an example of the former, I'd offer up AT&T's long running *Reach out and touch someone* advertising. For years, this advertising did a wonderful job of connecting people with the emotional marvels made possible by a long-distance telephone call. Worked like a charm. Until one day, a certain MCI snuck up behind it and literally bush-whacked it with its own sweet "reach out" message, when one of the performers in a wonderful lampoon of the AT&T spots ended with the statement, "*Have you **seen** our phone bill?*"

The other peril inherent in pursuing Connection with too much of a vengeance is airing heavily right now. It's for a product called Rozerem, which is apparently a prescription sleeping aid. The thrust of the advertising is, *Your dreams miss you.* Okay so far. But then the advertising attempts to connect with its audience by showing some examples of those dreams. And maybe I'm unique in this regard, but I have never, ever had a dream that featured Abraham Lincoln and a muskrat sitting around my kitchen table with an astronaut standing in the background. Yes, I know, this advertiser is just trying to stand out and have a little fun, perhaps. But the imagery is so bizarre, all Connection is lost (they're not speaking to *me*), along with a good deal of Credibility (bizarre imagery for a prescription product), and Comprehension, too (huh?).

Putting it all together

So as you can see, it's important to evaluate any communication on the basis of *all* 4Cs of Truth in Communication. No one of them will do the job by itself, although each C offers you the opportunity to flourish or flounder. Get three of the four right and you're not doing too badly. But get all four and you're on your way to effectively communicating.

In fact, this is a belief I like to challenge just by applying the 4Cs to communication I'm exposed to as a regular citizen, not something I've been asked to evaluate professionally. I might apply the 4Cs to something I just happen to see or read and then attempt to predict how this particular communications approach will fare in the long run.

Recently, I had a great experience with this. I was watching television and a commercial came on that featured two individuals, one looking kind of like a small town CPA, slightly overweight and dressed in a tweed jacket. To counter that character, the other actor was dressed all in black, pretty hip (but not over the top), with a more contemporary haircut, day-old stubble, and so forth. And these two individuals start talking as if they are actually computers, one (guess which) representing the world of PCs and the other, the world of the Apple Macintosh. They banter back and forth about some particular feature—virus vulnerability, ease of use, and the like. At the end of the commercial, the nerdish character falls to the floor, unable to stand the forward motion and innovation being addressed by the "cool" guy.

Not surprisingly, my 4Cs antennae went up like a shot. Comprehension? Couldn't have been clearer which computer came out on top. Connection? No question. All of us, even the PC users in the crowd, could relate better to the cool guy than his foil. Credibility? Once again, even as a PC user, I have to admit to having a tad more faith in anything Apple has to say relative to innovation and creativity than what the Microsoft/PC world offers. After all, Apple invented the iPod for goodness sake! And as for Contagiousness? Well, the spot was clever, the characters were appealing, each in his own role, and the message was clear and engaging.

In my mind, based on the 4Cs, this was a campaign that was going places. And sure enough, six months later, there are new executions every month, each one better than the last. Of course it probably doesn't hurt that this campaign also has a couple of other Cs behind it, namely the famous advertising agency creative director, Lee Clow, and the highly enabling "cash" to ensure frequency and memorability.

Sometimes it just doesn't matter

I was presenting a paper on the 4Cs to fellow qualitative research consultants at our industry's annual conference recently and we got around to discussing the importance of one C versus another. One of my colleagues who I'm assuming does a lot of medical research, said that for most of her clients, Contagiousness is irrelevant. I guess it stands to reason that what's most important in medical/pharmaceutical communication is that the patient understands the product (Comprehension), feels there is a true need for it in their lives or that it will improve a specific condition (Connection), and that the manufacturer or physician making the recommendation is believable enough (Credibility) to make consumers feel safe about using the product. All of this made perfect sense to me. Whether or not the communication was exciting, made them think of the product in a new way, or was unique or different in any way would likely be much less important than the other three Cs.

The important lesson of this chapter is to realize that one C is not more important than another, just more or less relevant based on the objectives of the communication, the people it's trying to reach, and the condition of the marketplace at the time. In fact, as we'll explore in the next chapter, it's probably more appropriate to conclude that the sum of the 4Cs is greater than its individual parts.

CHAPTER 11

The Ultimate "C" Students

Truth persuades by teaching, but does not teach by persuading.

—Quintus Septimius Tertullianus

At this point I hope I've demonstrated how valuable the 4Cs can be at making all forms of marketing communications more powerful and thus, more effective. But that begs another obvious question: Are the 4Cs strictly a tool for evaluating and enhancing marketing communications or could they have far broader applications? Naturally, I'm biased, but the more I look around me, the more I see the 4Cs in action, even if they don't go by that particular name.

For example, take George W. Bush (I know, an easy target), who during the 2004 Presidential campaign was often disparaged for having been "only a C student" at Yale. Well, ironically his opponent was also a "C student" at Yale, but one of them vastly outperformed the other when it came to putting the 4Cs to work

Let's start with Comprehension. I know it's been awhile since the 2004 campaign, and the communication blunders, not to mention the strategic political mistakes, have been subjects of many other books out there. But think back, and try to recall which candidate's message was more easily comprehended? George Bush's right versus wrong, good versus evil, black-and-white world view? Or John Kerry's intellectualized, seeing both sides of the question, nuanced and shades of gray version? To me that's kind of a no-brainer.

Okay, and what about the Connection question? Well, it would seem to me that the candidate who consistently ranked higher as "someone you'd like to have a beer with" connected far more effectively with people than the one people might like to meet for cocktails at the yacht club. Both candidates were, in fact, trying to be themselves. The problem (for Kerry at any rate) was he came across as an aloof, almost snobbishly intellectual member of the elite, whereas Bush came across as a regular guy.

Then there's the question of Credibility, which in light of developments over the last few years, would seem to be a dodgy question. But going back to 2004, I think President Bush benefited enormously from his steadfast, some might say, bull-headed convictions. Sure, it might be a case of "often wrong, but never in doubt," but the fact remains, the Credibility of his platform overshadowed Kerry's shifting positions.

And finally, there's the matter of Contagiousness. In the political arena I think the best proxy for this is the alacrity with which a candidate is embraced. How many lawn signs did you see for Kerry versus Bush? Unless you live in Massachusetts, I suspect you saw more of the former. It was the same with bumper stickers, buttons, you name it. Bush supporters went to the polls with glee; Kerry supporters had to set two alarm clocks that morning. The result was almost a foregone conclusion. Of course, as I've been alluding to, I'd say at this point there's some communication reassessment in order. In fact, the direction that the Bush administration took since the election would imply a critical need for a 4Cs "emergency" assessment.

It's the economy, stupid

Lest you think I'm endorsing the Bush administration here, I'm neither endorsing it or bashing it. I'm simply pointing out that candidates who better understand the principles of the 4Cs are more likely to prevail and are infinitely more likely to distill their messages into phrases like the subhead to this section. Democratic strategist James Carville has an intuitive mastery of everything that lies behind the 4Cs— even though he's most assuredly never heard the term— and Karl Rove exhibits the same talent. And what about the colorful Richard J. Daley, who captivated the citizens of Chicago for four straight terms, serving as mayor longer than any other man in the city's history with his candor and clarity? The fact of the matter is the candidate whose message is the most easily comprehended, easy to connect with, credible, and highly contagious will almost always win. And sometimes the smartest people in the room, the Adlai Stevenson's of the political scene, will remain on the sidelines clinging to the nuances and subtleties of their arguments.

So are we all this easily spun? I know, on the surface, the 4Cs can seem terribly superficial. Are we really that susceptible to the way information is presented? Is the power of communications that powerful? Well, we're all busy human beings, with limited time and in many cases, modest intellectual firepower to bring to bear on all the aspects of a particular issue. Plus, to be honest, many of us have somewhat attenuated attention spans, to put it kindly. In this "over-messaged" (but decidedly "under-communicated") world we live in, all of us have the opportunity for Andy Warhol's "15 minutes of fame," but probably have less than 15 seconds to gain the attention necessary to get there.

Communication is communication

So maybe there is a role for the 4Cs in the political arena. What's that got to do with the 99.5 percent of readers who harbor no political aspirations whatsoever? Possibly a lot. Aside from the few Trappist monks who might be reading this, we are all in the communications business. With every PowerPoint presentation we create, every trade show booth we put up, every piece of sales literature we approve, every blog we contribute to, every speech we deliver, it's all communications and all subject to the same rigorous standards the 4Cs put forward.

In reality, the glib phrase "content is king" is dangerous, and if you ask me, a wrongheaded notion. Content isn't king; compelling content, or to use today's latest communication buzzword, "engagement" is king, and to get to that you need to score highly on Comprehension, Connection, Credibility and ideally, Contagiousness. Even as humble an everyday form of communications as e-mails, as discussed in some detail in chapter 9, could benefit from some scrutiny via the 4Cs. After all, what is that seemingly innocuous thing called the "subject line" if not a headline? That's precisely what it is. It might not matter if your boss or your most important clients only get two or three e-mails a day, but chances are they get more like two or three hundred a day and what you say in that subject line could easily dictate

- how soon it is read,
- with what degree of attention it is read,
- how quickly it is responded to.

And you thought only copywriters have to sweat headlines!

Then there's the not insignificant matter of websites. It's a given today that almost every business and certainly every corporation of any substance has one. But how do they perform under the 4Cs microscope? How comprehensible are most corporate websites? And how well do they make connections? Actually, one of the things I like to do with the 4Cs is see how readily these concepts translate into the common language of other communications vehicles.

For example, if I was consulting with a website development firm and I wanted to speak its language, I might say that *Comprehension* translates into, "ease of navigation." The more intuitive and user-friendly it is, the easier it will be for a viewer to understand and interact with it. *Connection* might be another way of saying "sticky." It seems like common sense to assume that if you like a site, if it seems to be finding common ground with you, you'll stick around a lot longer than you would on a site that's just seeing the world from its own, solipsistic perspective. Credibility is an interesting one, and I wonder if Google page rank doesn't send a strong signal here insofar as a site only gets a lot of page views if a lot of people feel its content is both relevant and reliable. Finally, there's Contagiousness, which if you ask me, can easily be measured in links. A site that's being passed along by lots of people to their friends and co-workers is, by definition, achieving a high degree of viral success, and you don't get much more contagious than the viral variety.

Going Hollywood

As much as I have no objection to applying the 4Cs to website evaluation or even conducting seminars where the 4Cs are applied to PowerPoint presentations or e-mails, I can think of few places where the 4Cs could have a greater impact than in the world of entertainment.

Take movies and TV pilots, for example. Some typical research methodology consists of holding screenings during which the attendees rate the film on a variety of levels using electronic tabulators they hold on their laps. Sounds like kind of an unnatural setting to me. Or in some cases, the industry is still handing out small, 3 x 5 -inch cards on which the attendees can essentially grade how much they "liked" the movie or pilot. It's not an entirely worthless endeavor to be sure, and many movies or TV shows have had radical surgery based on this feedback, especially to their endings and lead characters. But how much more helpful would it be if these forms of communication were subjected to the scrutiny and rigorous analysis of the 4Cs?

Thinking back to the 2006 Academy Awards presentation, we saw a lot of small-budget sleepers fare exceptionally well and a lot of big-budget "sure things" that ended up disappointments at the box office. Would the 4Cs have shed any light on that? I think they very well might have.

The best movie of 2005, *Crash*, and the best-directed film, *Brokeback Mountain*, were small movies about big and controversial subject matter. Think about how the 4Cs might have revealed their Contagiousness in early screenings. Early audiences, no matter what their feelings were about homosexuality, or cowboys, for that matter, could not help but walk out of *Brokeback Mountain* filled with mixed emotions and the very real need to talk about them, under the safely veiled guise of this provocative love story.

And talk about a Connection factor, the 4Cs would have certainly teased that out. Who hasn't experienced the feeling of undeserved pre-judgment of character or intention based on purely superficial evidence that was the dramatic cornerstone of *Crash*? And of course, getting the entire cast on Oprah, the ultimate catalyst to Contagiousness, to discuss the real-world prejudices displayed in *Crash* probably didn't hurt the Contagiousness factor of that movie either.

But what about those putative blockbusters like *War of the Worlds* or *King Kong*? Other than the apparently masterful sound editing in *King Kong*, for which it won an Academy Award, those movies fell far short of expectations. Could the 4Cs have foretold what the problems were with these expensive boo-boos and in so doing allowed the makers of these movies to do something about it? Pardon my matrix, but let's take a closer look.

FIGURE 11.1

The 4Cs of Truth in Communications Evaluation

	King Kong	*War of the Worlds*
Comprehension	Got it. I know the story.	Ditto
Connection	Didn't strike a chord because it didn't do anything better than the original—a classic, which I now think is much better than I used to think it was simply by comparing it to this new version! So here's a big clue. Didn't do anything to create a Connection with the viewer. "No, baby."	Ditto
Credibility	Well—the storyline, no. But hey, neither were intergalactic aliens drinking in a space bar, and that didn't hurt the success of *Star Wars*. What about the credibility of re-doing a classic? Sure, it's been done successfully many times (*A Star Is Born, The Getaway, Cape Fear*).	Ditto Yes—but. The aliens were much more technologically innovative in this one—and for me, somehow less intimidating.
Contagiousness	Yeah—but the bad kind. Reality did not meet the hype and expectations promulgated by the huge marketing machine that preceded the movie's debut and unavoidable comparison to the original.	Ditto. Plus some unfortunate timing of negative P.R. associated with the movie's major couch-hopping male star.

Since I'm neither a screenwriter nor a director, I can't begin to suggest how these movies might have been altered to achieve a different result. But I do know one thing: *knowing* that they were scoring poorly on one or more of the 4Cs is the key.

Clearly this 4Cs thing is quite the versatile tool. In fact, between its applications to ads, brochures, packaging, websites, and politics, it's beginning to remind me of one of those late night commercials for a Ronco product—you remember, "*It slices, it dices, it juliennes . . .*" So in the spirit of those indelibly ingrained commercials, I'll segue to my last chapter with the Ginsu Knife's famous refrain:

"*But wait, there's more . . .*"

CHAPTER 12

What Else Can U 4C?

Truth is the only safe ground to stand on.

—Elizabeth Cady Stanton

It seems like the best way to end this little journey we've been on is to look at not only how far we've come, but to also briefly explore how far we might go with the 4Cs. In terms of how far we've come, I think you will now agree that the 4Cs provide a useful tool for evaluating the effectiveness of many forms of communication—not just marketing communication, but business communication, political communication, communication in the form of entertainment, and just plain old everyday person-to-person communication.

But I've always felt the ultimate test of the effectiveness of this thought-corralling technique is two-fold. First, to what degree does it actually lead to better, faster decisions? I think that comes in constantly applying the method and getting really good at knowing how to use it and evaluate the feedback. And second, just how broadly can the technique be applied?

Well, let's try it. I could easily take the Boston Consulting Group's matrix and apply it to my dating years, which I didn't, but here's how it might have categorized things for me. I spent too much time on some dogs, had a few question marks along the way, and spent some time with a couple of cash cows (hey, even a dull dinner at Le Bernardin beats calling out for Chinese). And luckily, I found my "star," Ken. Now if only the process had been that deliberate.

So I thought, if my contention that communication is so central to everything we do, and the 4Cs process is so good at improving communications, maybe the final challenge would be to see how it performs in the areas that *really* matter. Those life situations that in the final analysis totally overshadow our success at making effective marketing communications, getting elected to office, or producing a hit movie.

He (or she's) just not that into you

I'll be profoundly grateful if this book sells a tenth as many copies as the entertaining one that bore this title, but it would seem that the entire area of relationships is one that remains in desperate need of communications therapy. And judging from myriad books out there on relationship handling, juggling, explanation of fractured relationships, and consoling when it's over, it would appear that we do need some assistance early on. Heck, from the titles alone, it seems that this is an area in dire need of establishing some effective communication assessment. Along with the title mentioned above, *He's Just Not That Into You*, by Greg Behrendt and Liz Tuccillo, take a look at some of these others and ask yourself if a little understanding of truth in communication might have precluded the need for some, if not all of them:

- *Why Men Love Bitches: From Doormat to Dream-girl—A Woman's Guide to Holding Her Own in a Relationship* by Sherry Argov

- *It's Called a Breakup Because It's Broken: The Smart Girl's Break-Up Buddy* by Greg Behrendt

- *Be Honest—You're Not That Into Him Either: Raise Your Standards and Reach for the Love You Deserve* by Ian Kerner

- *Stop Getting Dumped! All You Need to Know to Make Men Fall Madly in Love with You and Marry "The One" in 3 Years or Less* by Lisa Daily

- *What Men Won't Tell You but Women Need to Know* by Bob Berkowitz

Okay, so, how might the 4Cs of Truth in Communication address the ever-present conundrum of the male/female relationship? Starting with Comprehension, one might ask the question: Do the two parties involved or thinking about getting involved understand each other? Do they *get* one another? Are they sending out mis-interpreted messages or are they "crystal"? Do they have mutually compatible goals for the relationship? If their goals are unclear or widely divergent, that's something that might be helpful to know. As in *right now*. And it's not something one should assume would eventually be understood through osmosis or by just continuing to hang around together. The heart is only a lonely hunter when it, and the heart it is hunting, discover they're in two entirely different forests.

Connection in this case can be thought about as that emotional glue—that sense of "stickiness" that you feel when you "click" with someone. And we all know from comparing good and bad relationships that when there is a Connection, a spark, the relationship just "goes," as in hums along nicely or if you're lucky, sky rockets to the moon. When it's not there, it just "goes," as in, "off a cliff." Sooner or later, usually sooner, someone loses interest (*"he's just not that into you"*) and then what the other person says or thinks or does or wants doesn't really matter. There's really no point in carrying on, is there, when there's no Connection? And if you're honest with yourself, you pretty much know this right away. See how nicely this works?

As far as Credibility goes, this is a trickier one. Because there is a great degree of chemistry involved in any great relationship—there's that silly amygdala again—it's painfully easy to see what we want to see in someone we find attractive. But here's where I'd argue a little reality therapy, ably assisted by the 4Cs, could only help. You get each other. Great. You share the same goals. Terrific. You've completely connected with each other beyond just a physical attraction. The best. But can you both deliver? Are you really the person you've presented yourself to be? Or have you just pretended to understand his obsession with "breweriana"? (Which, by the way, has taken me fifteen years to do, but I finally do get it!) Do his actions follow his seemingly sincere proclamations? Is she really believable when she tells you she'll be there for you? And does she come through when it counts? All big and very important questions. And possibly those most likely to steer you clear of the deadly delusion that maybe you can change him or her. Of course, you know that's rarely possible. People don't truly *change*. They might evolve to become more acceptable to you over time, but basically we are who we were.

And finally, there's the matter of Contagiousness, which is just another way of asking: Even if you understand each other, click with each other beyond some superficial attraction, and have both proven your Credibility, how excited are you by one another and by the prospect of a long term relationship? Which gets back to how "into" each other you really are. So much so, that you feel "infected" by each other? That you want to shout out loud to anyone who passes by, "I dig this guy or girl!"? It's not important that you do this, of course, to satisfy Contagiousness—just that you *want* to do this. Everyone's estimation of excitement varies, and each relationship will have its own unique definition of Contagiousness, but I'd maintain if there isn't some degree of pulse-pounding flutter to the enterprise, if there isn't a vivid emotional response when you are in each other's presence, if he isn't "competitively differentiating" and most importantly, if the relationship isn't motivating you to *do something*, it probably falls into the category of "settling," something houses are built to do, but relationships generally aren't.

The 4Cs of parenting

I'm sure someone somewhere at some time has written a book called *Your Kids Just Don't Listen To You.* Or if not, someone should and I'm sure it would be a New York Times #1 Best Seller! I guess coming out of our discussion on relationships, this one is just the next natural progression to be 4C'd, although I'm thinking it's going to be the most difficult to execute because we're dealing with a lot of thick and sticky, emotional and heavily irrational connections. And of course, we are talking about children, who can be inherently exasperating! But if you're a parent, you can definitely connect with what I'm about to say. Because when you think about it, is there really any way for parents and children to truly *get* each other? As much as we tell our kids we've been in their shoes, they really can't imagine we've ever been anything but grown up. And even as adults, we have to admit that what things were like for us as kids, no matter when that time was, is not what it's like for kids now. Communication overall has experienced a sea change since we were kids. We did not communicate through instant messaging, e-mail, or text messaging. We used the phone, or more often, just walked down the street. For me, spending a good part of my childhood in the city, I would just call out my window to my best friend who lived in the building next door. We didn't even need a phone, but we clearly *got* each other.

Yes, communication has changed, to be sure. And anyone with a teenager knows that *getting* one another might be a futile effort no matter what! In our case, I'm hopeful, but not convinced, we may have a chance. But at least the

4Cs can help us all get on the same page. Here's an example. Your 11-year-old son calls out to you as he's pedaling down the driveway, "Mom, I'm going to Tommy's house and will be back in a little while." "Okay," you say, "but don't be away too long because we have to leave for Grandma's party." Well, right there you have compromised Comprehension with too many vagaries. "A little while." "Too long." Those can have widely different definitions to an adult and an 11-year-old. And of course, in my case, they did. "Mom, if you wanted me back in 15 minutes, you should have said 'come back in 15 minutes.'" He's right of course. My message was in bold violation of the Comprehension C on clarity. We were terribly late to my mother-in-law's party.

Remember how we talked about Connection being when something really *speaks* to you? In the case of parenting, it pays to connect. My teenager will work nicely here as an example. My 13-year-old daughter fancies herself a full-fledged teenager now. She's very happy to be there and she embraced the role very quickly. The eyes are rolling back in her head when I say something she perceives to be stupid, the responses to my requests have become just a little more sarcastic and take much longer to execute. That sort of stuff. I'm figuring I'm not connecting with her, not *speaking to her*, or more likely, what I'm saying doesn't really matter. The other day we were in the car together. I was driving and talking (okay, maybe slightly lecturing) about how high school is going to be much more academically and socially challenging than grade school. As I was talking, she was singing. I asked her, "Why are you singing when I'm talking to you?"

To which she replied, "I'm multi-tasking!" Yes, at that point in time, we were probably experiencing a Connection problem.

Remember that old, often used-parental adage, "Do as I say, not as I do"? My mother used to say that to me all the time. Even as a young child, I always thought that was a cop-out. Come to think of it, I'd be hard-pressed to find a better lead in to the Credibility area. Children are astute observers of the behavior of those around them. And if what a parent is suggesting is at complete odds with what the child observes in the parent's own behavior, how credible it that? I am only persuasive to my children in communicating the importance of going to church every Sunday, because I, in fact, go to church every Sunday.

And finally there's the Contagiousness aspect of all this. How truly exciting do your kids think your message is? Is it serving up something to them in a new or unique way? Is it "competitively differentiating"? That is, are you saying something to them in a way that is different than the way they've heard it from every other adult? Or, come to think of it, maybe it might all just come down to motivation. "What's in it for me?" For some kids, it may be a financial incentive. "Clean your room every day this week and you will get your allowance." This is very clear communication, I think. And motivating. They are presented with the potential of a direct pay off. For both my 8-year-old and 11-year-old sons, anything that has to do with sports or sports paraphernalia will work nicely, whether it's withholding or granting. Whatever the motivation, whatever excites them and generates some sense of energy, if we are truly communicating with our children, there has to be a certain amount of Contagiousness about what we're saying, or else we get tuned out. A little simplistic, maybe. But most of the parents we know don't have a lot of time for complicated solutions. This is just a simple way to illustrate that no matter the subject or target of communication, the 4Cs can provide a quick assessment of that communication.

So there you have it

I know for a fact that the 4Cs work for all forms of marketing communications. They work for organizing and assessing all important aspects of consumer communication, for deconstructing what's working and what isn't and thus paving the way for radical improvement. I've seen it happen many times when applied to everything from ad headlines to positioning concepts to menu boards and package graphics. And I think this chapter begins to construct a persuasive case for the 4Cs application to virtually all forms of communication between two parties.

If you'd like our help applying them to your brand's advertising, positioning, package or promotions efforts—or your company's corporate communication posture, employee relations communiqués, programming content, or convention speeches and agendas, we're ready. For personal relationships, parenting, and the like, I'm afraid you're on your own. But at least now, you've got a not-so-secret weapon. Congratulations and good luck!

Index

© Sorrells Signature Portraits

About the Author

Since 1999, Isabelle Albanese, a 23-year marketing and communications veteran, has led the highly regarded consumer insight-driven consulting firm, Consumer Truth,® Ltd. In this capacity, she and her business partner and former advertising agency veteran, Ken Quaas (who also happens to be her husband) have actively used the 4Cs of Truth in Communications™ model literally hundreds of times to objectively validate and optimize consumer response to the communications efforts of highly recognized and respected consumer brands including: Dove,® Suave, Avon, Dunkin' Donuts,® Lever 2000, Togo's® Sandwich Shop, Del Monte Foods, Ikea, A&E Television Networks, Quaker Life Cereal, Dollar Rent A Car, and Breyers® Ice Cream, as well as those of many other brands for advertising agency partners such as J. Walter Thompson, Foote Cone & Belding, Leo Burnett, Element 79, and Ogilvy & Mather.

She has presented the 4Cs of Truth in Communications model to rave reviews at international conferences among both client and colleague audiences, and through conducting upwards of 1,000 group discovery sessions, one-on-one interviews and in-home/on-site ethnographies, has developed an expertise for hearing and innately understanding consumers' truth.

Prior to starting Consumer Truth, she was a senior vice president at J. Walter Thompson Advertising where she spent 11 years in both their New York and Chicago offices, playing a key role in the strategic and communications efforts of leading consumer packaged goods brands such as Nestle, Helene Curtis (Unilever) Hair Care, Kraft Foods, and Warner-Lambert (Pfizer). Prior to that, Isabelle spent several years at the venerated Ted Bates Advertising Agency in New York in account management on the M&M Mars confection brands.

Isabelle has a B.S. in business from DePaul University and attended business school at DePaul and The University of Chicago. She is an active member of the Qualitative Research Consultants Association (QRCA). She lives with her husband in the suburbs of Chicago, and when not employing the 4Cs for client-related projects is actively engaged in the 3Rs and 3Ss (soccer, singing, and softball) with her three children. One of her favorite truth adages was written by Pearl S. Buck:

"The truth is always exciting. Speak it then. Life is boring without it."